BURN-OUT
The Super-Achiever Sickness

"Many men and women who come to me in pain report that life seems to have lost its meaning. Their enthusiasm is gone. They feel uninvolved, even in the midst of family and friends. Their jobs, which used to mean so much, have become drudgery with no associated feeling of reward.

"All their lives, they have undertaken tough jobs and prided themselves on their ability to master situations . . . a difficult child, an exhausting job situation or economic reverses. They had enough determination and will power to lick anything. Now, however, no matter how great their efforts, the only result seems to be frustration. Some vital spark inside these men and women is burning out, leaving a terrible void."

ARE YOU, OR SOMEONE YOU LOVE, BURNING OUT? HERE IS THE BOOK TO HELP YOU SURVIVE.

BURN-OUT

BURN-OUT

The High Cost of High Achievement

DR. HERBERT J. FREUDENBERGER
WITH
GERALDINE RICHELSON

BANTAM BOOKS
NEW YORK · TORONTO · LONDON · SYDNEY · AUCKLAND

This low-priced Bantam Book
has been completely reset in a type face
designed for easy reading, and was printed
from new plates. It contains the complete
text of the original hard-cover edition.

BURN-OUT
*A Bantam Book / published by arrangement with
Doubleday & Co., Inc.*

PRINTING HISTORY
*Doubleday edition published October 1980
5 printings through May 1981*

Serialized in NATION'S BUSINESS, WOMAN, HEALTH QUARTERLY,
January/February issue and DATAMATION, *July 1981*

Bantam edition / November 1981

ISBN 0-553-20048-8

Published simultaneously in the United States and Canada

Bantam Books are published by Bantam Books, Inc. Its trademark, consisting of the words "Bantam Books" and the por-
trayal of a rooster, is Registered in U.S. Patent and Trademark
Office and in other countries. Marca Registrada. Bantam
Books, Inc., 666 Fifth Avenue, New York, New York 10103.

PRINTED IN THE UNITED STATES OF AMERICA

Dedication

For Arlene, Lisa, Marc, and Lori,
whose affection and indulgence
serve as my fire alarms.

Acknowledgments

This book would not be possible without the many patients from whom I learned so much; the groups who helped me to keep my humanity; the staffs at the various schools and agencies where I worked. As specifically regards the creation of the book, I want to thank Myrna Gelman for making herself and her skills available at all hours. And a special thanks to Gerry Richelson for her creativity, probing questions, and insightful contributions.

Contents

Introduction

If you have ever seen a building that has been burned out, you know it's a devastating sight. What had once been a throbbing, vital structure is now deserted. Where there had once been activity, there are now only crumbling reminders of energy and life. Some bricks or concrete may be left; some outlines of windows. Indeed, the outer shell may seem almost intact. Only if you venture inside will you be struck by the full force of the desolation.

As a practicing psychoanalyst, I have come to realize that people, as well as buildings, sometimes burn out. Under the strain of living in our complex world, their inner resources are consumed as if by fire, leaving a great emptiness inside, although their outer shells may be more or less unchanged. Possibly you recognize what I am referring to in some of your own feelings. Perhaps you are disenchanted with the life you're living, but have never been able to put your finger on precisely what is wrong. If so, you are not alone.

Many of the people who come to my office describe similar feelings, and yet they are neither neurotic nor psychotic in the historical sense of those words. That they are suffering is undeniable. Their lives seem to have lost meaning; often they are unable to get along with family, friends, and co-workers; they are disillusioned with their marriages and careers; they are tired, filled with frustration, and forced to put forth increasing amounts of energy to maintain the pace they have set for themselves.

When I realized how many of my patients' stories had a common thread, I began to listen to what they were saying in new ways. Soon I recognized a phenomenon at work that had less to do with a childhood trauma than with a relatively recent malaise. Many of these people had gone along for years coping with life in a positive fashion. Housewives, for instance, who were alarmed to find themselves popping Valiums or drinking in the late afternoons, had long-term records of accomplishment behind them. So did executives who were currently neglecting their jobs for extra-marital affairs. So did many students who were dropping out. Whether in parenting, studying, loving, or working, these assorted types had started out with high expectations and visions of achievement. For most of their lives they had been enthusiastic, energetic, optimistic. Then gradually, what I term "dulling and deadness" had set in. The energy had turned into ennui, the enthusiasm into anger, the optimism to despair.

Why? These men and women had certainly put forth plenty of effort, yet the harder they worked and played, the more stubbornly satisfaction seemed to elude them. And not just in a handful of cases. Almost every day someone would sit across from me and describe feelings of emptiness and disappointment. The theme was appearing in movies and books. Even in cartoons. Just recently, I came across a drawing in *The New Yorker* of two women chatting over a drink, one saying to the other, "I got what I wanted, only it wasn't what I expected."*

Many times, I heard statements like that from my patients, mixed with their other thoughts. I began to compile data and chronicle experiences. Soon patterns began to emerge. If I were to construct a typical composite of what I was hearing, it would sound something like this: "I came from a pretty good home, I went to school, settled into a career, married someone I loved, had children. We're a pretty successful family. Money,

---

*Wm. Hamilton, *The New Yorker*, October 23, 1978.

home, cars—but something is missing. None of it seems to matter. And I'm tired of working so hard."

Nothing crazy about that. But a lot of pain. A lot of exhaustion, disillusionment, and in many cases, a failure to function. These men and women were exhibiting signs of something amiss between themselves and their environment. As a group, they had committed themselves to active, involved lives, and along the way, they had started to burn out. In talking to some of these people, as well as the staffs of the clinics and agencies where I was a consultant, I began to use the term "Burn-Out," and each time I did, I got a profound reaction. Immediate identification. "Yeah, that's how I feel. Burned out."

The more I studied, the more I came to realize that Burn-Out was robbing our society of what it could least afford to lose: high-achievers, the men and women of action and purpose to whom the rest of us looked for leadership and inspiration. These were not failure-oriented or habitually self-destructive people. On the contrary, they were the ones most likely to succeed. In such a group, what was happening could not merely be something inside of them. Much had to be attributed to the times we live in, the swift acceleration of change, the depersonalization of neighborhoods, schools, and work situations.

My Story

One of the prime motivators of my probing examination of Burn-Out was my own experience with it many years ago. Although at that time, it had been a nameless episode in my life, I now recognized it as the equivalent of what so many of my patients were going through. It had happened during the sixties when I was working in the free-clinic movement as well as continuing to maintain my private practice, family life, active membership in professional organizations, and other commitments. At that time, large numbers of young people were dropping out and getting into the drug scene, wandering around Haight-Ashbury in San Francisco and the East Village in New York, broke, scared, and sick, with no place to turn for help. Like many of my colleagues, I wanted to do something to help them; perhaps because I had been a child in Nazi Germany and had survived only by a miracle and a support network that included many strangers, I was even more eager than others.

Without beginning to understand the magnitude of the problem, I opened a storefront clinic in the East Village. A few young social workers and psychologists volunteered their time as did a few young doctors, but for the most part, the staff was recruited from the streets and in need of training. From 8 to 6 each day, I took care of my regular practice, then rushed downtown to the clinic until we closed the doors at 11 P.M., when we held our staff meetings and training sessions. At 1 or 2 A.M. I was heading for home. The more tired I was, the more I pushed myself. When my wife tried to caution me, I responded with irritation. "You think I should be doing less? I should be doing more. There are thousands of these kids, and they have no other place to turn. When I get there, the steps are overflowing with them, waiting for me, hoping to be able to talk to me. If I worked around the clock, I couldn't do enough."

Had I paid attention to my own words, I might have spared myself much misery later on, but I was obsessed with making the clinic work. Had I taken a good look at our facilities and what was going on there, I would have realized that I had set an impossible task for myself. We didn't even have a well-equipped infirmary, just a filthy, unrentable store and good intentions. There were thousands of children. Most of them were addicted to drugs. Some overdosed, others took bad acid trips. There were pregnancies, venereal diseases, malnutrition. During this period, not only wasn't I listening to myself, I wasn't listening to anyone. When people I ran into who had not seen me for a while told me how bad I looked, I would get annoyed and reply, "I'm fine. Never felt better."

"But you're so thin," they would insist, and I'd retort

with something flippant like, "So's Frank Sinatra," and get away as fast as I could. My patients were noticing the change in me. Every day I would get a few personal questions. "You all right, Doc?" "Everything okay at home?" "How's the family?" In truth, I hardly knew how the family was. I was seldom home and when I was, the children gave me a wide berth. Although I wasn't aware how combustible I was, they were, and they stayed as far away from me as possible. At the office I was irritable, often flying off the handle and scolding people for not getting better faster. At the clinic, I overidentified with the kids. Their problems, their battles became mine and I began to lose my objectivity, which is the last thing a helper should do.

Things continued this way for many months as I continued to deny that anything was wrong despite my lingering cold, my fatigue, and my constant irritability. During the Christmas holiday my wife insisted that we take a vacation with the children, and much as I hated to be away from the clinic, I felt I should go to make up for all the time I had spent away from home. My wife made the hotel and plane reservations. All I had to do the night before we left was pack my own clothes, but when I dragged myself through the door at 2 A.M., I was too exhausted to do anything except fall into bed. I told my wife that I would pack in the morning, but in the morning I couldn't get up. We never got to the airport. I slept for two solid days and ruined the family vacation. On the third day, I was still not able to get out of bed, but I *was* able to begin reflecting on how I had been behaving.

I quickly realized that I had generated a strange episode in my life, one that was quite uncharacteristic of me and even stranger because through it all, I had been on a runaway course that all my training and expertise had not been able to stop. It was obvious to me now that I had to do something more than just spend a few days in bed. I had to find out why I had become so fanatical about the clinic, working like a madman twenty hours a day, neglecting my health and my family in the process. I decided to talk about the experience

into a tape recorder to see what I could learn. My plan
was to talk each day, put the tape aside, listen to it the
next day, and then talk some more.

When I heard the playback of the first day, I was
startled to hear my voice. It revealed a complex of
emotions that I hadn't noticed: exhaustion, anger, depression, arrogance, and when I talked about my family, guilt. I continued with the tapes, talking at random
every day, determined to analyze myself and find out
what my underlying motives had been. It was easy to
see how I had exhausted myself: No one can work at
such a fever pitch for as long as I did and not wear
himself down. What had led me to do it? Why had I
been so intense about the clinic that my judgment had
become impaired? What was I feeling at the time? What
was I proving? I was filled with recriminations, but I
forced myself to put them aside and plan a constructive
program for myself. I stayed home during the vacation
period catching up on my sleep and spending time with
my family. I allowed myself only two items of work:
talking into the tape recorder and writing an article
about my experience. The tapes gave me important insights and the article served as a catharsis.

I stayed away from the clinic for a full month. I felt a
sense of loss, but I knew I couldn't go back until I had
re-established my priorities and could place my work in
the clinic where it belonged—after my family, my
health, my patients, my obligation to earn a living. If I
returned before finishing the tapes, I was likely to be
thrown off balance again. As it was, every part of my
life had been affected. I had to take precautions against
slipping back. I had to teach myself new ways of looking at my work and dealing with it. It was a slow process, doubly difficult because I was so exhausted, but
gradually I began to feel healthy and whole again.

As I continued to analyze the tapes, I saw that my
experience at the clinic was triggered by a combination
of forces, many of which I could not control—the sheer
number of children, the inadequate physical plant, the
lack of trained personnel, the lack of sympathy from
the general community. Some of the forces, however,

were internal. Because of my own early personal experiences, I was particularly sensitive to the conditions of homeless youngsters. Even before I opened the clinic, I overidentified with the "flower children," imagining great similarities between their plight and the nightmare of my childhood in Germany. Now I could see how off base I had been. These young people were not being pursued by Nazis, nor were they struggling to reach a safe destination. The circumstances that had caused them to be homeless bore no resemblance to my memories and required new solutions, which I might have found if external conditions hadn't compounded the problems.

Do you have a sense of depletion, of being burned out? Is something wrong with the relationship you're in? Does the position you worked so hard to attain seem meaningless to you now? Do your children seem restless and remote? Are co-workers goofing off? Is the organization a maze of red tape and foul-ups? Are friends no longer as stimulating? Do you seek increasingly dangerous diversions to bring a sense of liveliness or joy into your life? Would you like to pack it all in and run away?

If you find yourself nodding your head to some of these questions, it's time to start looking for answers. Although you may never have let it surface, somewhere deep down, buried under all the layers of "What's wrong with everybody?" lies a more important worry, namely "Maybe something's the matter with me." Well, maybe there is. Maybe you're showing signs of a Burn-Out, and if you are, there's a lot you can do about it. In the course of this book, you will have an opportunity to take a fresh, dispassionate look at the feelings that have been disturbing you. You will be able to delve into the causes of your discomfort, examine your symptoms, look at this complicated world we are living in, and get your life back on track.

What I most hope to demonstrate by an in-depth look at Burn-Out and its manifestations is that whatever you are feeling now, you can soon feel better. Burn-Out signals not despair but hope. Recognized and attended to, it can become a positive energy force, signifying that the time has come for a cease and desist action, a hard look at yourself, and a change to something new.

As you read about other Burn-Outs who have been able to turn their lives around, and answer the questions throughout the book, absorb the information. You will get insights into yourself and the people close to you. The very knowledge that what seems to be a lack of love or caring is in reality a symptom of other problems can be astonishingly therapeutic. Whether you are involved in someone else's Burn-Out or your own, take heart. In every fire, there are glowing embers. You can use them to rekindle the spark.

The Phenomenon of Burn-Out

❧

Have you ever awakened in the morning unable to sleep any longer and equally unable to get out of bed? You lie there for a few minutes, trying to remember why you woke up in the first place, what it was you were supposed to do.

"Ah yes," you think, "work. I have to go to work. But wait, maybe I don't have to go today. Maybe I can call in sick."

Then, one by one, you count off the urgencies . . . the appointment at ten, the report you promised, the meeting at two. You throw back the covers. The day has begun.

You hope, as you jump into the shower, that the splashing water will wash the heaviness away, and your old vital, energetic self will emerge. What leaves the house instead is a grim, unsmiling figure, a little bent, a little tired, lips and shoulders set against the irritations of the day ahead.

And for that figure, the day *will* be irritating. There will be too much work, too many interruptions, too many details, too few rewards. The day will be marked by fatigue and tension. And even the ending of it will bring no moment of exhilaration, because it's not just work. Even family, friends, and social situations have become "weary, stale, flat, and unprofitable."

If you recognize yourself in that picture, you're probably wondering how you got that way. Where's that old dynamic you who used to start every day with enthusiasm and vigor? Why is the life you embarked on with

1

such high expectations letting you down at every turn? Why does it seem you have gotten what you wanted only to find you don't want it?

Take heart. There *are* answers to those questions. And chances are, you don't have to spend years searching back through all the stages of your life to find them. They may be more readily available than you have been led to believe.

More than likely, if you've been functioning well in the past and have seen yourself progress from one level of development to the next, you're not suffering from some deep-rooted psychological problem. You may not need to dig for traumas and other significant events of long ago to explain your decreasing ability to function or to care. That nameless malaise with its physical symptoms, its feelings of depression, anger, and weariness may be a developing case of Burn-Out . . . a demon born of the society and times we live in and our ongoing struggle to invest our lives with meaning.

THE TIMES WE LIVE IN

Historically, the American dream has been to rise above what one's parents were; to work hard, even play hard; to achieve excellence, which would in turn lead to material comfort, community respect, position, prestige, compliments, security, status. This has been the American dream both for its people and for the nation. In short order, the United States formed itself, sprawled, grew, invented, discovered, industrialized, and surpassed every society of history in wealth, material goods, and self-esteem. We enjoyed more prestige and envy than any other nation. The goal of the world was to come to America to find gold in the streets and freedom in the air.

Why, then, with all these goals and visible rewards, which we as Americans have accepted so unquestioningly, has the result been a singular lack of satisfaction? Why are so many of our best and our brightest beginning to feel empty and unfulfilled? Why does it seem there must always be more accomplishment, more achievement, more effort? WHY, AS A NATION, DO WE SEEM, BOTH COLLECTIVELY AND INDIVIDUALLY, TO BE IN THE THROES OF A FAST-SPREADING PHENOMENON–BURN-OUT?

Many men and women who come to me in pain report that life seems to have lost its meaning. Their enthusiasm is gone. They feel uninvolved, even in the midst of family and friends. Their jobs, which used to mean so much, have become drudgery with no associated feeling of reward.

Usually these people have come most reluctantly to seek professional help. They are accomplishers and doers who have no room in their philosophies for what they consider weakness. All their lives, they have undertaken tough jobs and prided themselves on their ability to master situations. Whether it was a bad marriage, a difficult child, an exhausting job situation, or economic reverses, they would find a way. They had enough determination and will power to lick anything. Now, however, no matter how great their efforts, the only result seems to be frustration. Some vital spark inside these men and women is burning out, leaving a terrible void.

THE IMPACT OF CHANGE

We are living in times of change so rapid they've left us without moorings. Think of the roller coaster as it plunges headlong to the bottom. You've plunged along with it, but your system hasn't. Your head snaps, your body lurches, you're giddy and breathless, your stomach is still at the top. You tense yourself to keep up with the ride, but you tingle with a sense of weightlessness as if vital parts of you have been flung away. In a way, you've passed yourself by. Exciting . . . and more than a little scary.

Not too different from what we've been living

through since World War II. These have been remarkable times, moving forward at breakneck speed. We have probably seen greater change in the past few decades than in all the rest of history. Like the roller coaster, it's been exciting. But for many of us, a little too fast.

Think about it. Restraints and taboos have been swept away. In sexual mores alone, we have moved a millennium in about a quarter of a century. The mother who was herself raised to preserve her virginity until her wedding night and who had to observe curfews and bring her dates home for inspection now visits her daughter at college and finds a live-in boyfriend. Obviously, this causes all sorts of conflicts in the mother and, perhaps not so obviously, in the daughter, too. No matter how defiantly a young woman may protest her right to live the way she wants to, she cannot completely have shed the attitudes she learned in her mother's home. Somewhere inside of her, though it may be unconscious, a tug-of-war is taking place between the customs of her contemporaries and the teachings of her childhood.

A generation is a very short time span for learning to live with such a prodigious change. Whoever coined the term "sexual revolution" was deadly accurate; our world went to sleep one night and awoke the next morning having undergone a drastic transformation. And not only in our sexual behavior. Within that same time span, communities have broken down. Divorce has become a commonplace. Women are redefining their roles. Technology has bombarded us with new ways of doing things. Affluence has brought us more leisure than we know how to handle. The credit card seduces us into buying by promoting ready cash. Education has placed us on new plateaus that make us discontent with simpler life-styles. At the same time, TV has exposed us to alluring pictures of people leading the "good life." We're finding, as Alice did in *Through the Looking-Glass,* that "it takes all the running you can do to keep in the same place. If you want to get somewhere else, you must run at least twice as fast as that."

Yet if Oliver Wendell Holmes was right (and I believe he was) when he said, "a man's education begins a hundred and fifty years before he is born," we can begin to see the dilemma. We are products, not of this culture alone, but of two conflicting cultures. Within us, the past dies hard. No matter how hedonistic the world may be at the moment, it was pretty puritanical not so long ago. Our parents raised us on *Poor Richard's Almanack* and similar dicta that go all the way back to the Old Testament and exhort us to strive, accomplish, and observe the Ten Commandments.

When we stray from these guidelines, we feel uncomfortable and guilty, yet when we follow them, they don't seem to pay off. Others, who are breaking all the rules, appear to be flourishing while our own lives are dull. *We* don't cheat on our taxes or buy hot typewriters, yet we know many who do, and they neither get caught nor suffer from guilty consciences. While we're still driving our beat-up, six-year-old Chevy on our way home to our family, they're passing us by in a Mercedes, starting out on a swinging evening. All the fun is "over there" somewhere, just outside our grasp. Very disturbing, since according to everything we've been taught, we should have been rewarded. Somehow, there's a great contradiction between reality and the messages we've been receiving, and we end up confused. I believe it is this climate of confusion that has given rise to the phenomenon of Burn-Out.

In a society where we have killed our gods, exorcised our ghosts, separated from our parents, and left our neighborhoods behind, we have little left to cling to. Against what restraints do we forge our standards? According to whose values do we plan our lives? The old rewards and punishments have disappeared. We have to rely on ourselves and ourselves alone. Not an easy task. If we want to fulfill the responsibilities we have accepted, we have to close our ears to the siren's call. Without any longer being sure of what is right or wrong, we have to resist temptation on every side.

Such an effort requires a constant buildup of defenses. Without even realizing it, we spend a lot of time erecting structures that can protect us. As we pile layer on layer, the weight bows us under. We begin to make excessive demands on ourselves, all the time draining ourselves of energy. To compensate for the weakness, the burning out we feel, we develop a rigidity. Things must be just so; the slightest deviation causes pain. Our accomplishments must become ever worthier to prove the rightness of the exhausting struggle. To maintain our position, we must constantly excel.

Unfortunately, the harder we try, the more we impair our efficiency. About the only thing we succeed in doing is burning ourselves out more. If we do achieve our goals, we find little pleasure in them because we're too tired to enjoy them. So our efforts end in disappointment; our attitudes in cynicism. Our resources exhaust themselves. Our endeavors produce nothing.

BURN-OUT: WHO'S PRONE?

In everyday language, especially when it's applied to mechanical objects, Burn-Out is a very common term. If we're working in the backyard with a power saw, and it suddenly gives off a burst of sparks and stops running, we realize the motor has burned out. Same thing with a light bulb when it goes "pooft" and leaves us in the dark. We know precisely what has happened.

Unfortunately, however, when good old reliable Paul suddenly tells the client to shove it, or June, a successful career woman, starts coming back from lunch a little tipsy, we don't really know what's going on. We are not familiar with the concept of Burn-Out in human beings, so we look elsewhere for answers. If we are personally affected by the erratic behavior, we react with anger or hurt feelings, punishment or withdrawal. We may decide the person is anything from a "goof-off" to a "pain in the ass," an ingrate to an eccentric, or someone who lost what he once had. On the other hand, if *we are* the ones who are erupting, we will quickly assign the blame to something or someone outside ourselves. Our self-perception, our own self-image, does not allow us to contemplate that what is going wrong may be a function of factors within ourselves.

Emily's Story

These numerous denial reactions are doomed to make a bad situation worse. Take the case of Emily, a young woman caught in the maelstrom of reconciling the two sets of mores her generation had been exposed to. She and her husband met in college and married soon after graduation. They settled in Chicago, where they both found good jobs, he with a drug manufacturer, she with a public-relations firm. The two salaries allowed them to live well, and in time they settled into a relaxed, sophisticated routine—dinner out when they wanted it, a nicely furnished apartment, good clothes, weekends away. Emily loved her job, which afforded her some travel and contact with glamorous people. She felt independent and accomplished.

As she approached the end of her twenties, she found herself thinking about children. Her husband, Richard, wanted a child, and her parents never visited without asking when she was going to make them grandparents. Emily, herself, had mixed feelings about changing her way of life, but she made an agreement with Richard that he would help out and she could go back to work as soon as she liked. That's what they did. When the baby was six weeks old, they hired a housekeeper, and Emily returned to her job. Her boss was delighted to see her, and she was equally delighted to be back. She fell back into her office routine with a sense of renewed energy and purpose, determined to make up for her time away. Her work had never been better. She seemed like a fountain of fresh ideas and within a few months was promoted to a position of greater responsibility, servicing major clients and traveling more than she had before.

Although Emily wasn't noticing, the situation at home wasn't flourishing like the career. In the world of public relations, there's no such thing as a nine-to-five day. Frequently, events have to be held in the evening or in distant cities. Emily was seldom home, and when she was, she was too tired to be much company. Many evenings, she didn't see her husband and daughter at all or she was "too beat to eat" and wanted nothing more than a hot bath and bed. At first, Richard was accommodating, pitching in with the baby and the meals. He knew how much Emily's career meant to her, and besides, he felt honorbound to abide by the agreement they had made before her pregnancy, especially since he had wanted the child more than she had.

As time passed, however, he couldn't help feeling neglected. Emily had become more like a mistress than a wife; more like a visiting aunt than a mother. He tried subtle ways of telling her, but they only served to make Emily defensive. "Gee, Richard, I get enough pressure on the job," she would say. "I don't need grief from you. Besides, it won't go on forever. Things will settle down soon."

But things didn't settle down, and Emily showed increasing signs of strain. She vacillated between *not* doing and overdoing. When she felt guilty about her absences from home, she'd compensate by leaving the office early and taking over from the housekeeper. On those evenings, she attended to her daughter's supper, bath, and bedtime, and expected Richard to praise her for her efficiency. Because she was so tired all the time, her judgment was impaired, and she honestly couldn't see how difficult she was being.

Things finally came to a head one evening when Richard had an important business meeting and Emily had promised to be home by six-thirty. At five o'clock, her boss called an emergency meeting, and the next thing Emily knew, her watch said ten to eight. She flew out of the office and into a cab, prepared to make apologies and have Richard accept them. But not *that* night. As she opened the door, Richard was standing there with a look on his face she never remembered seeing before. "You are, without a doubt, the most inconsiderate woman I have ever known," he let fly. "Night after night, I sit in this house alone, taking over for you, and the one time I tell you it's important, you don't show up." Emily was horrified. Richard went on and on, spewing forth all the grievances he had been collecting. "Do you realize how selfish you've been?" he finally concluded.

That, of course, was the last thing Emily was likely to realize, and she rushed into their bedroom in tears, accusing him silently of being petty and jealous of her success and no better than the other "male chauvinist pigs" she had read about. Over the next weeks she refused to discuss the incident, and the distance between them increased. Finally, when Richard insisted on a confrontation, she said she wanted a trial separation. She left him with the child and moved in with her friend Gretchen. "He thinks he's doing it all without me. Let him find out," she told Gretchen, expecting a sympathetic ear. "He said I could go back to work, and no matter how tired I was, I never complained. Most nights, I did everything for the baby, and I paid the housekeeper out of my salary. For a year now, I haven't done a thing but go to work and run home to be with him and the baby. I haven't shopped or had my hair done or even gone to the dentist. And *he's* feeling neglected. He's behaving like a two-year-old."

Gretchen, who had known Emily and Richard for a long time, was astonished at Emily's view of things. In Gretchen's mind—and in the minds of most of their friends—Richard had behaved like a saint, indulging Emily, being supportive, and never complaining although she had clearly been taking advantage of him. Gretchen felt she couldn't let that speech pass without saying something. Trying her best to be tactful, she said, "Emily, sit down. Let me fix you a drink. I want you to listen to a couple of things, and I want you to listen with an open mind. I think you're making a big mistake, Em. Richard has been pretty terrific through all this."

"Uh-oh," Gretchen thought, as Emily started to get up from the couch. "Not tactful enough." But Gretchen wasn't one to give up easily, and she put her hand on Emily's shoulder to keep her seated. "No, Em, I want you to hear me. You and Richard made an agreement that you could go back to work. I know that. But be fair about it. You didn't just go back to work. You plunged into a twenty-four-hour whirlwind and stopped being a person, let alone a wife and mother. You don't have to tell me you haven't gone shopping or to the hairdresser. I can see that for myself. But what I also see—and apparently you don't—is that you've been tyrannizing Richard with this 'male chauvinist' crap. He's gone all out to consider your position. Do you honestly think you've considered his?"

Emily was furious. She was truly convinced she had leaned over backwards to consider her husband and child, so much so that she was exhausted from the strain. If Gretchen couldn't see that, she must be blind. Come to think of it, Gretchen always did have a soft spot for Richard! She, Emily, had been a fool to come here. She'd pack that night and go to a hotel.

Emily was reacting in the classic way of a Burn-Out, denying her own contribution to a bad situation and exhibiting signs of paranoia. In her eagerness to be the model "New Woman," she had become rigid in her defense of herself, insisting that her view of the situation was the *only* view. Instead of listening to Richard and Gretchen, who were merely asking her to examine her behavior, she accused them of plotting against her. Then, to justify that accusation, she invented a romance between them, twisting the facts to suit herself and attributing Richard's understanding of her business trips to his desire to be with Gretchen.

Emily was so far along in her Burn-Out and was clinging so hard to her image of herself, she was incapable of seeing that she had lost her priorities and her humanity. Consequently, everything she did compounded her problems instead of ameliorating them. Had she not been so defensive, Emily would at least have considered the questions Gretchen had raised. Why couldn't she get to the hairdresser? Other working women did. Why did she have to say "yes" to every assignment that came up? Did her career really depend upon her being available round the clock? Did she have to be the "Wonder Woman" of her profession?

Emily had set up impossibly high work standards for herself, based partly on a deeply entrenched family principle ("Whatever we do, we do it well.") and her misguided notions of what women's liberation was all about. Even without a husband and child, she couldn't have lived up to her standards, as she was shortly to find out. Nobody is Wonder Woman. Everyone needs balance, and Emily had let her life become totally lopsided. Misguidedly, she had given herself permission to neglect the most important part of her life when she should have been curtailing her work effort. That, however, would have been an admission of weakness in her mind, whereas she was able to reconcile herself to the failure of her marriage by blaming it on Richard. By leaving him and the child, she thought she was ridding herself of the source of her conflict, but in reality she was tipping the scales even further. When, less than a year later, her Burn-Out became critical enough to force her to take a leave of absence from her job, she was shocked, although no one else was.

BURN-OUT: WHAT IS IT?

A person who is burning out is not, on the surface, a very sympathetic figure. He or she may be cranky, critical, angry, rigid, resistant to suggestions, and given to behavior patterns that turn people off. Unless we're able to probe beneath the surface and see that the person is really suffering, our tendency will be to turn away. Sometimes, like Richard, we'll bottle up our own hurts and frustrations just to keep the peace, but that doesn't work, either. The earlier we approach a Burn-Out, the more hope we have of eliciting some understanding; the longer we wait, the more defensiveness we're likely to encounter. That's true even with ourselves. As we saw with Emily, we'll go to any lengths to deny we're burning out. Just as she transferred her shortcomings to Richard, we'll look for anything or anybody we can blame. We look away from ourselves in an effort to cover up.

Burn-Out, however, is not a condition that gets better by being ignored. Nor is it any kind of disgrace. On the contrary, it's a problem born of good intentions. The people who fall prey to it are, for the most part, decent individuals who have striven hard to reach a goal. Their schedules are busy, and whatever the project or job, they can be counted on to do more than their share. They're usually the leaders among us who have never been able to admit to limitations. They're burning out because they've pushed themselves too hard for too long. They started out with great expectations and refused to compromise along the way.

I've never met a Burn-Out who didn't start with some ideal in mind. Perhaps it was a marriage that was going to be like the marriages in the storybooks. Or children who were going to be the "family jewels." The list is endless. A talent. A cause. A position in the community. Money. Power. A meteoric career. Whatever. A Burn-Out experience usually has its roots in the area of a person's life that seemed to hold the most promise.

Often, Burn-Out is the consequence of a work situation in which the person gets the feeling he's batting his head against the wall day after day, year after year. The helping professions are a good example. Many young, idealistic students who want to do something for the world become doctors, nurses, lawyers, social workers, policemen, teachers, counselors, politicians. They hope to have an impact on the lives they deal with. They envision making people well again, improving world conditions, turning wasted lives into productive ones, or sending educated students into the world.

Unfortunately, the helping professions get to see a lot of failure and misery. Doctors and nurses see their patients suffer and die. Teachers face overcrowded classrooms and students with a disdain for learning. Social workers battle against the overwhelming odds of poverty and hopelessness. The people they're trying to help are likely to have surrounded themselves with impenetrable walls. The disappointments mount up until eventually the helpers build walls of their own.

Since it hurts too much to care, they tend to anesthetize their feelings and go about their daily routines in a more mechanical and cut-off way. They're still conscientious and hard-working, but they're no longer functioning as whole human beings. In a slow, corrosive process, they remove a vital part of themselves. What happens is similar to what happens in a car that's running on only two cylinders—the cylinders that continue to function have to do a lot of compensating. After a while, the strain becomes too great, and something has to give. In the car, that something may be critical parts of the engine. In a person, it is usually other areas of his life.

A Burn-Out is "someone in a state of fatigue or frustration brought about by devotion to a cause, way of life, or relationship that failed to produce the expected reward." Stated another way: *Whenever the expectation level is dramatically opposed to reality and the person persists in trying to reach that expectation, trouble is on the way.* Deep inside, friction is building up, the inevitable result of which will be a depletion of the individual's resources, an attrition of his vitality, energy, and ability to function.

HOW DOES BURN-OUT BEGIN?

In a word, slowly. No matter how suddenly it seems to erupt, Burn-Out is a chronic condition, something a person has been working toward over a period of weeks, months, even years. Although we may be startled by the sudden flare-up that seems to come without warning, that flare-up was long on its way. There are circumstances such as cramming for an exam, pressure to get a project done, moving one's home, an illness of a family member, where a short-time-span Burn-Out occurs. Otherwise, Burn-Out is seldom acute. Often we don't notice it in its early stages because most Burn-Outs are competent, self-sufficient men and women who hide their weaknesses well.

George's Story

George is a good example. My introduction to him was a frantic telephone call from Kennedy International Airport, where he had just landed from a business trip abroad. He had been given my name by a former patient and had carried it in his wallet for months. Now, he had to see me immediately. It couldn't wait. He was going crazy. When we finally sat down a day later to talk, I found myself facing a good-looking, well-dressed man in his early forties who didn't seem crazy to me.

George impressed me as a take-charge type, agitated at the moment, but certainly lucid and articulate. He seemed too keyed up to sit, so I didn't stop him from pacing restlessly back and forth across my office while he spoke and chain-smoked. He had quite a story to tell. As the director of a large multinational corporation, he had been traveling through Asia and Europe on a tough schedule. One month. Sixteen countries. At each stop, meetings and conferences with high-level government and corporate officials. For George, it was a routine trip, part of the job. Except for one thing: the time element. Whereas his usual trip lasted two weeks, this one had been scheduled for four.

When the plans were being made, Hank, a fellow executive and good buddy of George's, had suggested delegating the last few stops to a subordinate. But George had adamantly insisted he could handle the meetings better and the schedule wouldn't bother him. George prided himself on being able to do most things "better," and he certainly seemed to have boundless energy. He had always taken on tough jobs for the company, had been willing to move his family every few years, and had climbed the corporate ladder quickly. On a business trip, he would go from the plane to the first meeting, put in a day that included lunch and dinner appointments, then go out at night. In Paris, he had a long-standing relationship with a woman, and although he had to be discreet, he always managed to make time to see her.

The trip went well. George and his staff had covered fifteen of their sixteen stops and reached London. Then the funny thing happened. George sent his bags to his hotel and made his way to a private, twenty-four-hour gambling club. "I might be there yet, Doc, if Hank hadn't located me. I think he called every number in London."

George was in that club for more than forty-eight hours. He played for a little while, then ordered a drink and dozed off in a chair in the lounge for what he thought was a catnap, but was really several hours. When he woke, he went back to the tables and kept repeating the process. He not only gave no thought to his carefully scheduled meetings, he didn't even know he had lost two days. The club had heavy drapes across all the windows, and in the enclosed space with only dim, artificial light, a sense of timelessness had overtaken him. When the transatlantic call came through, he was startled to hear Hank asking, "What the hell happened to you? The office is ready to call Interpol."

On the plane trip home, George was a very frightened man. He knew something was terribly wrong, although he couldn't decide between "coronary" and "crazy." He was so agitated and exhausted; he had severe pains in his chest. Fortunately, since nothing similar had ever happened before, there were no repercussions at work. His bosses treated the matter rather indulgently, as if it had been an adolescent peccadillo. There were a lot of jokes about orgies and sexual prowess. Only Hank and George knew how different the episode had really been.

WHAT HAD BEEN GOING ON?

For quite a few sessions, George held steadfastly to his belief that this incident had come out of the blue. There had been no previous signs, he said, no warnings that he was headed for trouble. That was what had made it so frightening. But as we continued to delve, a lot came out. George had been forgetting things for quite a while. Little things, like did he send that memo to the chairman of the board in time? Had he called to cancel his lunch date? Did he ask X or Y to follow through on a program? What did he promise to do for A in Tokyo? Was the order coming through in February or in March?

Sometimes, he found he had made two appointments for the same time. Once, he had left some dictation tapes, which he had worked until midnight to finish, in a taxi. The envelope had no name on it, and the tapes were completely lost. A picture was beginning to emerge. Then, very reluctantly, he told me about the sleeping pills, about how, especially on those hectic trips, he would get so charged up during the day, he couldn't get to sleep without them.

As we continued putting the picture together, George was able to acknowledge more and more. His irritability, for instance—he had been blaming his secretary for his inefficiencies. His impatience—all those times lately he had lashed out at his staff. His anger—that terrible incident at home when he had pulled the telephone out of the wall because his teen-age daughter had been talking for half an hour.

Despite the flamboyance of his London blackout, it had been anything but sudden. In fact, had he been willing to listen to Hank months before, George could have saved himself a lot of anguish. Hank had tried many times to warn him.

Before we look further into George's story and trace what had brought him to such a critical point, let's stop for a minute and look at you. Give yourself some time in a quiet place, away from people and pressures, and see how you've been acting and reacting lately. There may be many signs you haven't noticed that indicate you're headed for a Burn-Out. Notice them now. Let yourself become fully aware of what you're doing. Remember: Before you can begin changing direction to get back on course, you have to know where you are.

Later, we'll look at the whys and wherefores and hows of what brought you to your present point, but to get started, it's important to assess what's going on with you *right now*. The questions that follow will help you look at yourself. I'm going to restate the definitions of Burn-Out so you can answer the questions within the context of whether or not you *are* burning out.

BURN-OUT: TO DEPLETE ONESELF. TO EXHAUST ONE'S PHYSICAL AND MENTAL RESOURCES. TO WEAR ONESELF OUT BY EXCESSIVELY STRIVING TO REACH SOME UNREALISTIC EXPECTATION IMPOSED BY ONE'S SELF OR BY THE VALUES OF SOCIETY.

Look at the definitions again, and as you do, keep some of the key words in mind: "deplete," "exhaust," "excessively striving," "unrealistic expectation." See how they feel when you apply them to yourself.

ARE YOU BURNING OUT?

Look back over the past six months. Have you been noticing changes in yourself or in the world around you? Think of the office . . . the family . . . social situations. Allow about 30 seconds for each answer. Then assign it a number from 1 (for no or little change) to 5 (for a great deal of change) to designate the degree of change you perceive.

1. Do you tire more easily? Feel fatigued rather than energetic?

2. Are people annoying you by telling you, "You don't look so good lately"?

3. Are you working harder and harder and accomplishing less and less?

4. Are you increasingly cynical and disenchanted?

5. Are you often invaded by a sadness you can't explain?

6. Are you forgetting? (appointments, deadlines, personal possessions)

7. Are you increasingly irritable? More short-tempered? More disappointed in the people around you?

8. Are you seeing close friends and family members less frequently?

9. Are you too busy to do even routine things like make phone calls or read reports or send out your Christmas cards?

10. Are you suffering from physical complaints? (aches, pains, headaches, a lingering cold)

11. Do you feel disoriented when the activity of the day comes to a halt?

12. Is joy elusive?

13. Are you unable to laugh at a joke about yourself?

14. Does sex seem like more trouble than it's worth?

15. Do you have very little to say to people?

Very roughly, now, place yourself on the Burn-Out scale. Keep in mind that this is merely an approximation of where you are, useful as a guide on your way to a more satisfying life. Don't let a high total alarm you, but pay attention to it. Burn-Out is reversible, no matter how far along it is. The higher number signifies that the sooner you start being kinder to yourself, the better.

THE BURN-OUT SCALE

0–25	You're doing fine.
26–35	There are things you should be watching.
36–50	You're a candidate.
51–65	You are burning out.
over 65	You're in a dangerous place, threatening to your physical and mental well-being.

Who Suffers from Burn-Out?

❦

Not every personality is susceptible to Burn-Out. It would be virtually impossible for the underachiever to get into that state. Or the happy-go-lucky individual with fairly modest aspirations. Burn-Out is pretty much limited to dynamic, charismatic, goal-oriented men and women or to determined idealists who want their marriages to be the best, their work records to be outstanding, their children to shine, their community to be better.

These are the people who are dedicated and committed to whatever they undertake. And yet, dedication and commitment are, in and of themselves, positive life forces. A person who feels a true devotion to a situation or person, usually feels good. He or she goes about his or her activities with a sense of purpose and well-being. His or her energy level is high, and so is the accompanying sense of accomplishment.*

When trouble sets in, it is usually a result of *over*commitment or *over*dedication, and that, in turn, is almost always an indication that the person's goals have been externally imposed. Somehow, he embarked on his present course because it was expected of him. Or because a standard was set quite early which the individual accepted before he was equipped to think it through. He was never the authentic source of his

---

*In the interests of a smoother flow of ideas and a less cumbersome manner of writing, we will, from here on, confine ourselves to the masculine singular pronoun, wishing, however, that the English language provided a more satisfactory way of incorporating both sexes.

choices, and consequently, they afford little real satisfaction. Thus we see the search for more and more achievement and, ultimately, the Burn-Out. We all know of the "perfect" marriage or the "most spectacular" career that seems to get better every day and then, to everyone's amazement, suddenly goes up in smoke. If we could go back to the beginning and examine the people involved, we would probably uncover a combination of bad choices and good intentions.

"THE PERFECT MARRIAGE"

Philip and Doris's Story

Philip and Doris certainly started out with good intentions. They met in high school and were attracted to each other because of their similar interests. From the moment they began going together, everyone considered them a very special pair. Unlike many of their friends who had nothing much more than the senior prom on their minds, both Philip and Doris had hobbies that they intended to turn into their life work. Philip could do remarkable things with wood, and by graduation he was well on his way to being considered a master carpenter; Doris designed and crafted jewelry which some of the local shops sold for her on a consignment basis. By their senior year, they had each saved quite a bit of money, and no one in town was surprised when their engagement was announced.

Their parents approved, and their friends' parents held them up as a good example, saying such things to their children as, "Why can't you be more serious like Philip and Doris?" It was a commonplace in town for young people to hear, "Oh I hope things work out for you the way they did for Philip and Doris. Those two have so much in common. They're a perfect couple." By the time of their wedding, the "perfect couple" had much to live up to, and they did. Like the classic case of the actor who believes his press notices, they were as much impressed by their portrait as the people around them were.

They practically made a fetish of togetherness. They opened a shop and continued their crafts side by side. Philip made display cases for Doris's jewelry; she helped him arrange his wood pieces to show them off to their best advantage. In the evening, they'd go home to the small house they had bought and busy themselves with projects. He was building bookcases for the living room; she was hooking rugs for the walls. When they finished one thing, they'd go on to the next, hardly ever taking time off for a movie or an evening with friends. Before the marriage, Philip had bowled once a week and played softball on Saturdays. Now he preferred to stay home, and so did Doris. They were always cordial to friends who dropped into the shop or whom they met at an occasional wedding, but they seemed happiest off by themselves. Anyone could see they doted on each other.

A few years passed, during which Doris got heavier and Phil began to drink beer, first in the evenings, then more and more during the day. Nothing was wrong, exactly, but nothing was exciting, either. They didn't seem to have much to talk about, and they seldom bothered to have sex. While people were still saying things to each other like, "I wish you'd learn a thing or two from Doris. She's always talking about how wonderful Phil is" or "Why can't you be more considerate? Like Phil. He always helps Doris with her work. He even waters her plants when she's busy," Doris was alone in the bedroom masturbating and Phil was drunk in front of the TV set.

What a contrast between the myth and the reality! And why? Because Doris and Phil had put all their energies into a make-believe world where perfection is possible, and unfortunately, that's the only kind of world where it *is* possible. In the real world, people have faults and irritating habits, couples often have dissimilar interests which they pursue alone, and above all, people need to replenish themselves in order to have something to give. But Doris and Philip never ventured into the real world, nor did they let anyone into their "paradise," so eventually the perfection crumbled into boredom and monotony. For eight years they had allowed themselves no growth and had continued to operate on an adolescent level. The outward show, including all the loving talk, was a matter of habit and contained no substance whatsoever.

When the marriage blew sky high with Doris becoming a devotee of a guru and going off to join his commune, shock waves reverberated throughout the community. "Not Philip and Doris!" everyone said. "How can that be?" But the question was backwards. What people should have been asking was, "How could it have been otherwise?" Nobody can live in a fairy tale, and although Philip and Doris had begun with good intentions, they had stifled themselves with a series of bad choices. Here was a couple who had started out with more than most couples ever acquire—interests and goals in common, similar backgrounds, and a genuine fondness for each other—then applied these ingredients to a fantasy rather than chaneling them to promote growth. Had they not been trying to outshine the rest of the world, they'd have disagreed once in a while, even quarreled. They'd have cultivated outside interests and continued to see their friends. As it was, they spun themselves into a cocoon that smothered them.

Basically, the bad choice Doris and Philip made was to dedicate themselves to perfection. That is life's most exhausting endeavor and is always doomed to fail. Since everything was perfect, they could never air their grievances. Not that they had actually made such a pact; it was simply understood between them. Consequently, their resentments lay simmering beneath the surface until they erupted in an explosion. When Doris first started to put on weight, Philip was disturbed. He had a real aversion to heavy women and found them a turn-off sexually, yet he never expressed this feeling to Doris. If the subject came up, he would handle it in the artificial fashion they had cultivated toward each other, saying something saccharine like, "You're still my Doris. Prettiest girl in town." But at bedtime, he'd either be watching an old movie on TV or be fast asleep when she came to bed. By devoting themselves to a shiny surface, they let the foundation crumble, and the marriage burned out.

Two of the significant ingredients of Burn-Out are dedication and commitment, often affixed to an ideal or standard that is unrealistically high. Doris and Philip were extremes, but they weren't unique. Many couples try to fit their marriages into an unrealistic mold. Think how many beautiful pictures are painted for us in storybooks and movies. Think how many "musts" and "shoulds" and "oughts" we're given from the time we're old enough to listen.

Not that all imperatives and standards are wrong. Without them, we'd have no direction at all. If we had *no* guidance, *no* role models, we'd flounder and probably never get anywhere. It's only when demands become excessive and have nothing to do with the individual's true desires or needs that they become oppressive. Some families, perhaps because of a healthy measure of inner confidence, have a knack for striking the right balance between directing their children and allowing them to find their own self-expression. Other families seem to be setting traps all along the way.

BE CAREFUL: IT'S A TRAP

One of the commonest pitfalls for the growing child is the family hero. The "Why can't you be more like so-and-so?" syndrome. Sometimes the example is a long-suffering mother. She's never been well since her first pregnancy. But she doesn't complain. She cooks and cleans and does the laundry. She's there waiting for you after school every day. She'd rather see you get a new coat than have one for herself. "Your happiness makes me happy."

The hero might be a hard-working father. No education. No advantages. Possibly not even from this country. But he "buckled down" at an early age, and he's always been a good provider. It might be an outstanding brother, a good sister, or someone a little farther removed. Perhaps a successful, hard-driving, tough uncle or grandfather. A pioneer grandmother. Or an accomplished aunt.

Nancy's Story

Nancy was a victim of the last one. She had been named after her mother's sister, a brilliant woman . . . or at least, remembered that way. The aunt had been an accomplished pianist with a promising career ahead of her, but had unfortunately died in her late twenties. Nancy bore not only her name, but also the burden of having to fulfill the promise her mother remembered so well. Nancy was always being regaled with stories about her aunt. How dedicated, bright, and talented she was. How unusual as a person and what a loss to the family and society.

When Nancy was four, her piano lessons started, and she dutifully practiced, although as she got older, she came to hate and dread having to perform for her mother's guests. She was becoming proficient at the instrument, but knew in her heart it was because she was pushed to practice so hard, not because she had any innate talent. Same thing at school. Aunt Nancy had been a good student, so her niece struggled to get good grades, although she found the work difficult and didn't want to go on to college, which she knew would be more of the same.

By the time I met Nancy, she was fifteen and in the throes of a full-fledged nervous breakdown. She had completely stopped functioning, was a flagrant truant, and had painted the windows of her room black to blot out the day. Nancy's parents were totally perplexed and beside themselves. It had all been so unexpected. Nancy had been doing so well. They were sure she had been happy throughout her childhood and had recently fallen prey to some bad influences they didn't know about. Of course, had they been looking beneath the surface, they would have recognized many early signs— sadness, reticence, medical blackouts, unnatural fatigue, beginning abuse of alcohol.

THE REAL SELF AND THE IMAGE

It may seem that Nancy's parents were distant, insensitive, and uncaring, but that wasn't the case. They genuinely believed they were giving their daughter the best of everything. They paid attention to her, praised her, took an interest in her activities. The mistake they made was, unfortunately, a very common one. They were looking, not at the real Nancy, but at the image Nancy represented. And Nancy, eager to please them and hungry for the approval they lavished upon her, half believed in the image herself.

When she had thoughts about quitting her piano lessons, she pushed them away. Not only didn't she express them to her parents, she was unable to express them to herself. It was easier not to feel well—to have a headache or an upset stomach. That was something everyone could understand and would allow her some freedom from the demands. On a conscious level, Nancy convinced herself she was committed to becoming like her aunt, but because the goal was unrealistically high, she was systematically burning herself out. When the conflict between her true self and her image became too severe, the explosion occurred.

What's unusual about Nancy is that the image collapsed while she was still so young. Most of us prolong our images until much later in our lives. In George's case, it held up until that crucial, whirlwind business trip. But the underlying dynamic was the same. For years, both Nancy and George had been buying their images. They were their own best salespersons, locking their true selves away until they screamed to get out. To the world, George was charismatic, dynamic, inexhaustible, supercompetent. And the world wasn't wrong. To an extent, George *was* all those things. But only to an extent. Deep down he had needs, just like the rest of us. But because he believed in his idealized image, he had lost touch completely with his other, more fallible self. That meant George could never make a mistake or admit to being tired. He couldn't allow himself to ask for help, but had to deny his needs. He had to keep making greater and greater efforts as he became more and more exhausted.

Perhaps, like Nancy and George, you have occasional flashes that life has become one huge burden, that your calendar is fuller than you can handle. But because of habit or expectations, you push those thoughts away and drive yourself forward. This is a good time to let those flashes form themselves into pictures.

A GOOD, HARD LOOK INSIDE

First, think about your image, that competent *you* others have come to expect so much of. Think about your schedule, the tasks you perform, your family's expectations, your own expectations of yourself. Get a pad and write a short vignette of the "you" the world sees and hears every day. Then put your pad aside and close your eyes. Let that other *you* emerge. The real you that's tucked away beneath all those layers. The one you see first thing in the morning when you walk into the bathroom to prepare for the day ahead. The one you get brief glimpses of when you're all by yourself and feeling kind of beat. Now let that real you speak. Hear some of his or her feelings. And for once, listen. Don't shut that voice away. It may have important things to say.

There's a chance, the first time you look for this neglected part of yourself, that you won't get much of a message. The voice may come through a little muffled, the picture a bit out of focus. After all, it's been a long

time. It may take a few sessions to establish what is, in
essence, a new relationship.

Whether you get a lot or a little, however, turn to a
fresh page of your pad and write a second vignette.
Even if only fragments of thoughts came through, jot
them down. Whatever feelings you noticed—no matter
how fleeting—include them. They'll be important later,
and right now, they'll let you start comparing the two
"yous." As you get your first real look at the differences between them, you'll be taking a big step toward
closing the gap. And if you're on a Burn-Out course,
that gap has to be closed. Since being out of touch with,
or shutting off, large parts of yourself is a primary contributor to Burn-Out, your greatest protection against
it is self-awareness.

No one on the outside can effectively point out your
inner conflicts. Even the most skilled professional can
only guide you to seeing them for yourself. *You have to
be willing to look honestly and deeply and to incur
some pain,* but you'll be saving yourself a thousand
times more pain later on. As you continue reading,
you'll find many concrete measures you can take to
help yourself. But in order for those measures to work,
these excursions into self-awareness are imperative. The
more you know about yourself, the better. And if you
think you're ready to take a risk, there's one other thing
you can do right now: TELL SOMEONE YOU
TRUST ONE SMALL FACT YOU LEARNED
ABOUT YOURSELF. Share a nonperfection. If you
don't feel ready, just keep the possibility in mind and,
in the meantime, share it with yourself. If you think you
can try it comfortably, then by all means do. You don't
have to go into a lengthy explanation, nor do you have
to be overly revealing. Something as simple as, "I've
been doing some thinking, and I realize I'm very tired,"
will do. Or "I'm disenchanted." Or "I'm sad a lot
lately." Or "I'm getting little joy out of life." Or "I'm
eating too much, drinking too much, smoking too
much." Or whatever it is you're feeling.

Telling it will make it more real for you. And more
than likely, you'll feel a great sense of relief at having it

out in the open. The important thing is not to expect too much at first. Remember, the other person isn't familiar with this side of you, any more than you are. You may get a startled reaction or none at all, but that doesn't matter. What counts at this point is that you're letting the *authentic you* speak. You are pushing the image aside a little.

WHY WE BUILD THE IMAGE

Ironically, superimposing an image on our inner beings is our first purposeful act of self-help. When we decide to become something we are not, we make that decision for a good reason. We're not happy the way we are. Someone who matters doesn't love us enough. We're not getting enough attention. We don't have friends. We feel passed over or drab. Our perceptions may or may not be accurate, but it doesn't matter. That's the way we see it, and taking steps to do something about it can be a good idea.

Unfortunately, we're usually very young when we attempt to transform ourselves, and our actions are not guided by experience and judgment. The roles we assign ourselves may bring temporary rewards, but they're often not strong enough for the long haul. Look what happened to Nancy. By instinct, she was an "ordinary" little girl who would have been content to follow a nonspectacular path. But she became aware, before she had even started school, that that would never do. If she wanted her mother's affection, she had to be much more than ordinary. So she tucked her natural self away and brought out accomplishing, talented Nancy for the world to see and admire.

In Nancy's case the façade broke down because it was too burdensome for her to sustain. She simply didn't have that much ability. But many times, the image crumbles or fails to satisfy for a far simpler reason: *It no longer serves a purpose.*

Suppose, for example, your mother had been hospitalized for several weeks while you were about seven or eight. You were frightened, of course, and lonely even though your grandmother had come to stay with you and your two younger sisters. As the oldest girl, you were asked "to help Grandma." And you did. You showed her where things were, told her how your mother sorted the wash, set the table for dinner. When the baby wouldn't take a nap, you rocked her to sleep.

In the evening, when your father came home, Grandma was full of praise for you. She told your father what a help you had been and how she couldn't have managed without you. Your father, in turn, hugged you a lot. He, too, was proud and said it would help your mother get well faster to know how you were taking care of things. Wow! What a terrific feeling. Nobody ever paid this much attention to you before—especially since your sisters arrived.

Such an episode could—almost without any conscious thought on your part—lead to the formation of the image. Instead of resuming your usual role when the crisis passed, you would continue to be "the little helper," taking on adult responsibilities and expecting the same praise you had initially received. Because of the cherished associations with the time of your mother's illness, you assumed your efforts were being appreciated even when people seemed to take them for granted. Eventually, this pattern would solidify into a habit and govern your behavior in every life situation whether or not it was appropriated.

In circumstances like the one outlined above, the pressure to "be something else" arises internally. No one else may even be aware of what is going on. And many other chance occurrences can trigger a similar response. A character read about or seen on television can make a tremendous impression. A case of hero worship on a friend or teacher may trigger a decision to become more like that "ideal" being. Sometimes a role shift occurs when a child feels threatened by a new sibling. The older child may notice that the more self-sufficient he is, the less attention he gets, while the helpless infant is always being attended to. So he'll revert to soiling his diapers or not feeding himself. If the ploy works, that perfectly capable child may create a lifetime of dependency for himself.

Often, even without the threat of being replaced by a new brother or sister, children find out quite early that they can get time with their parents only when they need something. If the homework is going well, they do it alone; if they are having problems, however, Mom or Dad will sit down and help. You can recognize these people—fully grown—in every office and a lot of homes. They're the ones who can never figure out how to load the dishwasher or the ones who have to ask three hundred questions before they can settle down to do a job. They may not suffer from Burn-Out themselves, but they contribute to it in everyone around them.

It's important to remember that creating the image was probably a good idea *at the time*. It filled some existing need. The trouble is the human animal is a creature of habit, and habits aren't easy to break. Like nail biting, role playing becomes so much a part of the person that he doesn't even know he's doing it. If we reviewed our lives every couple of years the way we check our clothes closets, we might discard outmoded behavior the way we discard outmoded clothing. But while we can be objective about our wardrobes, it's much more difficult to evaluate ourselves. So we keep wearing our protective cloaks long after the danger has passed and the clothing ought to have been discarded.

TRACING THE IMAGE

In the little notebook I hope you started a few pages back, start a new page and head it, "Early Messages and Protective Devices." Look back as far as you can. This takes some practice, and when you take your first backward glance, you may not get to the really early stages of your life. There are techniques you can use to help yourself, and I'll list some of them for you.

1. Always sit in a quiet place when you're about to have a few minutes of introspection. No radio or TV. If possible, no interruptions. It's important for the memories to keep flowing, and once they start, you don't want them to vanish at the sound of someone's voice or the ring of the telephone.

2. Make yourself comfortable, but not to the extent of helping yourself fall asleep. You've spent a lot of years keeping these parts of your past tucked away. Your mind has built up a strong habit of not looking, and it will summon up all its resources to support its habit. You'll find yourself getting hungry. You'll be perishing for a glass of water. Your bladder will be exploding. Above all, you'll be sleepy—so remain in a sitting position—and forego the easy chair!

3. Give yourself directions as if you were talking to someone else. State the instruction out loud, then let yourself respond silently. Each time, take a few minutes to give the answers a chance to materialize. If you don't get anything, go on to another one. Don't attempt the entire list at one sitting, but make a point of returning to it from time to time. Be sure to repeat the ones that have eluded you, but never force an image or a picture. Eventually, it will come.

Think of a time you were happy.

Think of a time you were unhappy.

Think of a time you were embarrassed.

Think of a time your mother praised you.

Think of a time your father praised you.

Think of a time you were punished.

Think of a time someone was proud of you.

Think of a time someone was ashamed of you.

Think of a time you were afraid.

Think of something you never told anyone.

Each time you finish one of these sessions—and they don't have to be long, a few minutes at a time will be productive—jot down some of the incidents you remembered. Then see if you connect any of them to a protective device. Suppose, for example, you had a flash of yourself in the first grade reciting a poem on open-school day. Your mind had gone blank. You couldn't remember a line. And there you stood in front of the whole school—parents, teachers, and kids—petrified with embarrassment, wishing you were dead. What did you do about that? Decide never to stand up in public again? Develop a stutter? Start to hate school and never do your lessons? Become a bully? Retreat into yourself?

Not every situation will prove significant. Nor will every reaction. But look at each of them. If it was a turning point for you, you'll know it. Your gut reaction will be immediate and strong. Stay with that incident a little while. Then, as best you can, put into words the pattern you developed as a result of it.

THE FAMILY MYTH

So far we've seen how the traps of emulating a hero or overreacting to a temporary situation can lead us down a path that separates us from ourselves. And those are not the only traps we're faced with when we're young. The myth of the family is another, equally insidious. Just as individuals build protective façades for themselves, so do groups, and since the members of the group pick up on the image and feed it back to each other, it becomes reinforced a thousandfold. Often, the strongest message we take away from childhood is "We are . . ." It goes something like this: "In our family, *we are* brilliant in school" . . . "successful in business" . . . "talented in music" . . . "good with our hands." The list is endless, and you can probably supply the particular conclusion you heard at home.

Traditionally, myths are created to explain a frightening or little-understood phenomenon. Every primitive society invented an angry god to account for thunder or an abducted maiden to explain away the dark days of winter, and the family myth has similar origins. We've all had relatives or friends who were "poor but proud," and who gave off a powerful sense of this, often to the discomfort of their guests. When you were at their home, even informally, and they served a cup of tea and a platter of cookies, it always seemed to be accompanied by an unspoken explanation: "See how well we make do? We may not have an expensive cake, but everything is on a tray, and those are linen napkins." What that myth accomplishes for them is to shift the emphasis away from the "poor" onto the "proud," the latter being a phenomenon they can live with more easily than the former.

A family myth is primarily bound up with what we, as a family, are, and it pervades the household in subtle ways. A child may never be given a taste of alcohol, but if he hears from the time he can remember, "We know how to hold our liquor," he will be likely to start drinking as a teen-ager. If he hears, "We are too smart to be caught cheating," accompanied by tales of how his grandfather amassed a fortune unscrupulously, he'll absorb the notion that he's entitled to get through college having someone else take his exams. Whether the myth is positive or negative, it's always a trap. The child is impressionable, and a family tradition is being handed down that he thinks he must uphold. Even when he begins to get contradictory messages—from inside himself, from school, from stories he reads or watches on TV, from an admired playmate, from other families he visits—that primary message is difficult to deny. Long after the original source has been forgotten, the sentiment remains as a spur to unrewarding behavior patterns.

FAMILY PRINCIPLES

Closely allied to the family myth are the principles families live by. Whereas the myths are involved with a state of being and are transmitted to the child by a general ambience in the home, the principles take a more active form. They're not left to pass on through osmosis, but are given out in the form of rules and regulations. The principles are actually dicta that every member of the family is taught, sometimes painfully, to follow. A patient of mine had been raised in a family where the guiding principle was, "We pull ourselves up by the bootstraps." Her father was a well-to-do pharmacist who was known in the neighborhood as a charitable man. He never refused to help his customers, carrying some of them on credit, actually lending money to others. But he refused to send his daughter to college. *He* had gone to school at night, working during the day to accumulate his tuition money, and his attitude was that if she wanted the education, she could do the same.

It has been my experience that families have from three to five principles that govern their lives. "We sacrifice for each other." "We don't trust anyone." "We come first." If you can't live by those principles, you have a problem. By the time you are ready to leave that household, those guidelines will have been so thoroughly inculcated in your mind that they will rule you either directly or by denial.

In the sixties and seventies, when the rebellion of the young was at its height, we heard the "Establishment" and its institutions roundly taken over the coals. Young people dropped out of college, out of business, out of their parents' religion. They were vociferous in their distrust and repudiation of anything their parents had advocated. Yet all over the country, cults were springing up. The same voices that were condemning their fathers' rabbis, priests, and ministers were raised in praise of a guru. The very people who were proclaiming, "God is dead" were chanting "Hare Krishna" in the streets. And the tables of the young men and women who disdained their parents' dietary laws were now set with vegetables and nuts and not a trace of meat. Had these young people realized how closely they were adhering to the family principle, they would have been appalled. Although they believed they had left the family traditions behind, all they had done was invent new versions of an old motif, sort of a variation on a theme, but in spite of the new trappings, the family principle of living by religion remained intact.

Since a principle is more open and active than a myth, a principle usually produces a more overt reaction. The young rebels above were not simply rejecting their families' image of themselves as being outstandingly pious; they were thumbing their noses at the traditional observance their families had forced them to follow. Sometimes myths and principles are separate from each other. A family can perceive itself as deeply religious without abiding by a specific set of rituals; it can also abide by the rituals with no image of excessive devotion simply because it is a principle "in our family" to follow these customs. They were passed on by former generations and will be handed down to future ones.

Ambrose's Story

When a myth and a principle coincide, each reinforcing the other, the result can be doubly destructive. In Ambrose's family, religion was an all-pervading force, and all his childhood messages seemed to be centered on that one subject. "We are good, God-fearing people. We help others. We put ourselves second to God's work." Ambrose's mother would have loved nothing better than to see her son become a priest, but outside influences interfered. Ambrose was gregarious. He liked to play ball with the other boys and spend his free time with friends. He went to church regularly, but inside he was constantly impatient to get done with all that so he could be doing something else. Later, as sex began to make itself felt, Ambrose knew for certain he didn't want to go into the priesthood.

His mother was bitterly disappointed, although she needn't have been. She hadn't really lost the battle. Not by a long shot. True, her dream of seeing her son in a cassock hadn't been fulfilled, but her message had prevailed. Although Ambrose went into the business world, married, and started a family, he *thought* like a priest. He was always participating in causes, sponsoring programs for underprivileged children, coaching the Little League, doing favors for even the most casual acquaintances. By the time he came to see me, his wife was ready to leave him. Whereas he thought of himself as a Good Samaritan, she saw him as a doormat and a patsy, so indiscriminate in dispensing good will that he was neglecting her and their children. She also saw the extent to which he was exhausting himself and heading for trouble.

Since Ambrose wouldn't acknowledge any need whatsoever for him to see a therapist, his wife set up the initial appointments for herself and asked him to come along. He agreed most reluctantly and, for the most part, maintained a sullen silence while she tried to sketch a portrait of what had led her to come for counseling. When Ambrose did speak, it was to contradict or to trivialize something she had said. He was a master at twisting her meaning by focusing on irrelevant, minor details instead of the larger implications of a story. When she tried to make the point that the children hardly saw him anymore, he brought up a night, three weeks ago, when he had taken them out for ice cream. I could sense her growing exasperation.

One incident, which Ambrose recounted in a session at which his wife wasn't present, will give you the flavor of his life. A neighbor was going on a business trip and

didn't want to pay a parking fee for the few days he
would be gone, although he could well have afforded it.
He asked Ambrose to drive him to the airport, some
forty miles away, and Ambrose, "out of the goodness of
his heart," agreed. The plane was scheduled to leave at
6 A.M., so they were on their way before dawn. Ambrose drove the forty miles each way, returned the car
to his neighbor's garage, then left to put in a full day's
work.

That night he fell into bed without finishing his dinner, but when his wife tried to point out how unnecessary the whole affair had been, he answered with sanctimonious platitudes about serving one's fellow man.
The argument became heated, with Ambrose's wife
calling him a sucker, an idiot, and other assorted angry
names.

Ambrose was bewildered and hurt. "How can she be
so selfish?" he asked me. "The guy needed a favor.
And the Bible says, 'God loveth a cheerful giver.' "
There, in a phrase, was Ambrose's image of himself—a
cheerful giver.

But his wife didn't see his cheerful side. Nor was he
really so giving where she and the children were concerned. He had his priorities all mixed up. Also his
mentor. It wasn't God Ambrose was trying to please. It
was his mother. After all, the Bible also says, "Let them
first learn to show piety at home."

CONFUSION: THE ORIGINAL SIN

Ambrose is a clear-cut case of the confusion that sets in
early and haunts us throughout our lives until our defenses crumble and Burn-Out begins. In every Burn-
Out, there is an element of blindness, and in Ambrose's
case, it was nearly total. Not only couldn't he see what
his wife was talking about, but he had no notion of the
figure he was presenting to the world. Over the years,
he had become increasingly mechanical. He went
through his daily routines automatically, deriving no

pleasure from his activities and giving little pleasure. He walked like a zombie, holding himself rigid and moving slowly. His face was expressionless and made him seem stern and disapproving. He scarcely smiled. He was no fun to be with, nor was he interesting or spontaneous. Besides his willingness to be taken advantage of, he had nothing to offer. All that tension he was so determinedly hiding from himself was sensed by others to the point of turning them away.

Ambrose saw none of this. The only area of his life that concerned him was the physical. He was having trouble sleeping and even when he managed a few unbroken hours, he would wake up exhausted. He had begun to have aches and pains, but the doctors could find no specific ailment. He had been for a GI series, an electrocardiogram, a series of tests at a headache clinic, and he was sure that if only someone could come up with the proper diagnosis, all his troubles would vanish. He had been furious when his medical doctor suggested therapy and would never have come if his wife hadn't intervened.

After some weeks of trying to center our talks on the emotional side of Ambrose's life, I saw we would never make any inroads that way. Ambrose had been squelching that part of himself for so long it was completely buried. Whenever I asked him what he enjoyed doing, he would look at me blankly, like a stranger who didn't quite understand the words. "Enjoy" was not part of his vocabulary—a direct consequence of his mother's "priestly" message: "Do what you're expected to do. Be humble and good. Don't enjoy."

One day, when Ambrose was assailing me once again with his sleeplessness and lack of appetite, his headaches and chest pains, not to mention my incompetence, I decided to see if I could shock him into some kind of awareness. I took out a good-sized mirror and said, "Ambrose, you're kidding yourself if you think you're sick. You're dead, Ambrose. Dead. Here, look at a dead man."

That got us started. "Dead" was a hot button to Ambrose. He touched the mirror, but would not look into it, and he blurted out that he was afraid of dying and that was why he kept running to doctors all the time. I was able to point out to him, for the first time, that by sitting, walking, talking, and acting like a dead man, he was bringing about what he most feared. He was setting a pattern in motion and soon his body would follow it. It would get sick.

Ambrose reacted to this. I could sense the difference as he asked me solemnly what he could do, and I realized that at last he was willing to try. My first suggestions were very small. An hour or so playing ball with his son. Not strenuously. Just catch in the backyard. Enough to convince him he wouldn't drop dead from the exertion. Then gradually I made other suggestions. A movie with his wife. Something light that would give him pleasure. How about a cup of coffee after the film, so they could discuss what they had seen? This was very important. It had been so long since Ambrose and his wife had really talked, they needed an unself-conscious way to begin again. From there, we worked up to the two of them going out for dinner, so they could talk about real things without the pressures of their daily routine.

As you read, you may think how obvious those measures were, but at that point, nothing was obvious to Ambrose—neither his behavior nor the motivations behind it. He had to be spoon-fed every step of the way. His initial confusion about how to live had rigidified into a minimal survival act, and it wasn't until he began to open up in little ways that he was able to delve into deeper considerations. He had never had the slightest understanding of what it meant to be close to someone and relate in a meaningful way. The work in my office was similar to raising and teaching a child, because there was so much he did not know. Yet the world, as well as he, assumed he *did* know.

INTEGRATION: THE PATH TO ENERGY

At the beginning of this chapter, I described the typical Burn-Out candidate as "dynamic, charismatic, goal-oriented." If you're wondering how the Ambrose I've been describing fits that description, I don't blame you. Certainly, when he came to me, Ambrose was a far cry from an aspiring, accomplishing human being. But as he began to open up and discard the restraints he had been imposing on himself for so long, I began to see the Ambrose who had started out being all those things.

What's important about Ambrose's story is how separated he had become from himself. That's what had launched the Burn-Out in the first place, and as the Burn-Out had increased, so had the separation. First, Ambrose had merely suppressed his spontaneous feelings; later he snuffed them out completely. Together, we had to organize a hunt for that mischievous, fun-loving, gregarious boy of years ago. We had to reconstruct him step by step, actually reversing the process by which Ambrose had locked him away.

Because the family myth had been fed to Ambrose in such strong doses, he had superimposed the do-gooder value on his natural self, and for a long while it had worked. As a young man, he was still in touch with his fun-loving side, and the structure he had created disciplined him to do well in school and get started in the career he wanted. If was only as the new self became increasingly rigid that Ambrose had succumbed to Burn-Out. By the time I met him, he was truly "someone in a state of fatigue brought about by devotion to a cause that failed to produce the expected reward." Ambrose's cause was living up to his personal and familial expectations; the reward, as far as he could see, was nonexistent.

Ambrose had reached this state because he was totally run by his mother's message instead of by reality. He kept expecting to be rewarded for "being good," and deep inside he was afraid that if he relaxed and had fun, he would disintegrate. The "good" parts of him would crumble—and he would die. Eventually, as we worked together, he came to see that he needed both halves of himself, that one did not invalidate the other, and that he would be twice the person he was if he could let them exist simultaneously.

If you are burning out, even to a much lesser degree than Ambrose was, it is imperative to integrate the "you" that's been suppressed for so long and the "you" of the image. Although long ago they may have seemed incompatible, you will find now that they complement and bolster each other. Each one represents a valid side of you and can be a powerful source of energy. If half this energy is being used to suppress the other half, it's no wonder you're burning out.

When you looked at the two yous a little while back, you took a big step toward integration and vitality. Separation leads to Burn-Out, and Burn-Out is a killer of energy. You need your full supply to combat Burn-Out. By releasing the inner you, you'll be increasing your strength and authenticating your image. You'll be able to enjoy the many facets of your personality instead of using one to police another. Put another way, you'll be making it possible for yourself to use your image instead of being consumed by it.

The Feeling State of Burn-Out

∾

We have looked at some reasons why we build an image for ourselves. The hero. The family myth. Family principles. The secret belief that being different from what we are will lead to greater rewards. There are still other reasons, and we'll talk about them as we go along, but for now, let's detour and examine what it feels like to be burning out. When you answered the questions in the first chapter, you got some strong clues about the symptoms of Burn-Out. Perhaps you recognized several of them in yourself; perhaps you recognized only one or two. It's not always easy to see the signs, since they've been building up gradually over a long period of time. But one of the surest ways you can tell if you're burning out is to look at your energy level. If it is noticeably lower than it used to be, something is wrong.

CHRONIC FATIGUE

When all its systems are in harmony, the human body is a remarkable producer of energy. People who are enthusiastic about what they're doing can work for most of the day and half the night, get a few hours of sleep, then wake up refreshed, ready to begin again. Most Burn-Outs start out in life like that. They have so much energy, it spills over to the people around them. They are the spark of every project, the center of every group. They have that special attractiveness for others that we call charisma.

We see charisma most strikingly in some of our performers and political leaders. They may not, in a technical sense, be the best actors or singers or speakers, but they have a magnetism that draws us to them and makes us feel good. We refer to it as star quality and let it go at that. But if we look more deeply, we see that what we're responding to is energy in its most powerful form. To a lesser degree, we recognize this quality in some of the people we work with or meet socially. They're the Georges of this world. They exude confidence and competence, and it's an "up" to be part of their group.

People who are accustomed to having charisma and energy expect to have it continuously. They're not in the habit of accepting defeat or admitting to weaknesses, which is why it's hard to catch a Burn-Out in its early stages. These individuals cling to the belief that any exhaustion they feel is temporary. "Tomorrow," they think, "I'll be my old self again. Other people lose their strength. Not me." Realistically, however, strength is not something that exists in a vacuum. It has to be fed by something, and for the individuals we've been talking about, the important fuel is reward. When the rewards stop coming, their energy ebbs and Burn-Out begins.

If you, yourself, have always been a charismatic person, you know it. You never had to work at getting people to like you. They liked you spontaneously. You've always made friends easily. You've never lacked for love interests. At school and on the job, you've been a leader. Your efforts have been rewarded, and you've made rapid progress in any hierarchy. Once you start to burn out, however, all that seems to change. People bore you. Causes seem trivial. Whereas you used to participate at every meeting, coming up with plans and solid suggestions, you now sit silent, wishing you could get away.

Paradoxically, in the days when you *were* participating, the efforts you made served to exhilarate you. You used to leave those meetings all fired up to go back to your desk and get working on whatever had been discussed. Now, however, you leave exhausted, needing to get back to your office and close the door or even to go out for a drink. That exhaustion seems to follow you and affect everything you touch. You go to sleep with it. You wake up with it. It worries you, and at the beginning of Burn-Out, you try to deny it by working harder. People around you may realize you're not accomplishing anything, but you don't realize it. You feel abused and put upon and you blame your tiredness on your increasing workload. You begin to hate your job and your surroundings and everyone connected with them.

RECAPTURING YOUR ENERGY

If you feel your energy ebbing, there are things you ought to be doing about it. And one of the things you *don't* want to do is deny the fact the way George was doing before his European episode. If we go back to the concept of the *real you* and the *image* for a moment, we can reconstruct pretty accurately some of the dialogues that had been going on inside George's head.

REAL GEORGE: Listen, this is crazy. I don't want to make a whirlwind trip like this. I'm tired now, and we haven't even started. By the time we're halfway through, I'll be a total wreck.

IMAGE: Oh you! You've always been a drag. Everybody is counting on me to pull this off. There's no one else who can do it, and I'm not going to disappoint the whole company because of you.

REAL GEORGE: But . . .

IMAGE: But nothing. Maybe *you* can't do it, but I can. And I intend to.

* * *

Immediately—or as soon as possible—George's real self was squelched, and George was off again, playing hero, doing the impossible, denying his fatigue.

How many times have you had conversations like that with yourself? Think about them. Even if you can't recall whole sentences or complete thoughts, see if you can remember occasions when you were conscious of an internal conflict. A party, perhaps, when you felt like staying home but ended up going because "they" expected you to be a good sport, and part of you hated to disappoint them. Or maybe it was a school picnic, even though you had chaperoned the last two outings and had a million other things to do the day the picnic was scheduled. Yet somehow when the teacher said two of the mothers who had volunteered were sick and she knew she could always count on you, you found yourself saying "yes."

The secret to recapturing your energy is what George learned to do after he became frightened enough to change his ways: Listen to your real self. It's trying to tell you something. It may be speaking in a very small voice after having been repressed for so many years. But it *is* speaking. Before you plunge blindly into the next stressful situation, ask yourself if what you're about to do is reasonable. Is it your image saying "yes"? Or your whole self? Get those two yous into a conversation where they each have an equal voice. Integrate them by letting that hidden you come out into the open. Any other course will intensify the Burn-Out.

If you're afraid you'll become irresponsible or antisocial or inconsiderate of others, remember you're not innately that kind of person, so it isn't likely you'll do a complete about-face. If anything, you're now overdoing in the areas where you're constantly called upon to perform, and you have a long way to go before you reach the other extreme. If you don't start taking measures now, however, you'll stretch yourself to the point where George was. You'll go to one party too many, have one drink too many, and pass out. Or you'll lose your temper and spoil the entire class outing.

SEPARATION FROM ONE'S SELF

This matter of our two selves is so important I want to dwell on it a moment or two longer. On our paths through life, we have need for all kinds of coping devices, and a protective covering for meeting the world is certainly a valid one. I don't want to give the impression that one's image, or façade, should be totally stripped away. We're not made stronger or better by exposing all our weaknesses. Quite the contrary. If we're painfully shy, for instance, and meeting people causes us to cringe inside but we've trained ourselves to enter into conversations without stuttering, we're much better off. Similarly, if our natural impulse is to be impatient and cutting but we conceal that behind a façade of sociability, we'll gradually become less impatient, less cutting, and be better liked by others.

We don't live in a vacuum; therefore we need stratagems for fitting into society, and they serve us well as long as we're in control of them. It's only when our "Let's meet the world" façade pushes our authentic beings out of reach that the trouble starts. Then the distancing between what we are and what we seem to be becomes serious. Our values, our ways of functioning, our senses of morality, guilt, and justice all become skewed. We try to fit our real standards into our superficial selves without any success, until finally the real self gives up and turns to the other as its only hope for getting where it wants to go. At the same time, because the real self has been deemed worthless, the image needs more and more outside reinforcement to compensate for what it cannot get from within. Sometimes the superimposed image saves a troubled human being from something he considers abhorrent: someone of prurient interest, for example, who becomes a do-gooder and campaigns relentlessly against pornography and prostitution; the angry man who turns himself into Mr. Nice Guy; the gay who convinces himself he's straight. The world, given a choice, might opt for the hidden self (far better to have a tippler in our midst than a temperance fanatic!), but the individual involved despises it to such an extent that he has to go to the other extreme of whatever it is. Usually, he's fooling no one but himself and has to work so hard to maintain his adopted image that the very effort becomes the source of his Burn-Out. Covering up is the most important area of his life and the one in which he invests the bulk of his energy.

Helmut's Story

The first day Helmut came into my office, he put out his hand for me to shake, and as he did, he gave me a laughing warning. "Better watch out, Doc. I'm strong." That remark served as a prelude to Helmut's telling me all about his body building—up at six for an hour of calisthenics and weight lifting, half an hour at lunch on the walking machine he kept in his shop, a workout in the gym every evening. "You ought to try it," he advised me. "It would make a new man of you." To prove his point, Helmut took off his jacket and presented me with a bulging arm. "Go ahead. Feel that. Hard as a rock. And I turned forty-one last month."

Helmut talked constantly about his body. Exercising was only one part of his physical-fitness mania. He was also a nutrition nut, worrying about the purity of his diet to a nauseating degree. He bragged to me about unpleasant incidents at restaurants, including one where he lectured the waiter for putting a salt shaker on his table. "Boy, I really told him off," he said, gleefully. "He'll think before he salts his meat again. 'Poison,' I told him, 'that's what salt is. You're killing all your customers.'"

The rest of Helmut's life was vague in comparison. He had been married for "oh about twelve years." According to him, his wife was a bitch, "just like all the rest of them," but she didn't bother him much anymore. As long as he took her out to eat a few nights a week and paid the rent for their luxury apartment, she let him do pretty much as he pleased. Helmut was an upholsterer, and a good one, so his income was high. Since he and his wife had no children and she had always worked and paid for her own clothes, Helmut had all the money he needed for his activities. He went to the racetrack a few times a week, and he confessed to me that one of the reasons he was in my office was that he was afraid his gambling was beginning to get out of hand. "I used to bet forty or fifty bucks a day and go home satisfied whether I won or lost. Now I'm way up over a hundred. I always mean to stop sooner, but I really get off on it."

Gambling wasn't the only thing Helmut got off on. He told me long, ugly stories about how he'd go around looking for guys to beat up—in a respectable way, of course. Several times a week, he went for long rides on the subway or walks in the park, keeping an eye out for any black or Hispanic who looked as if he might be about to accost a woman. As soon as he spotted a suspicious situation, he'd walk up, grab the man by the lapels or the arm, and get to work. "This hoodlum bothering you, lady? Don't worry. You can go on your way now. I'll take care of him for you." If the man wasn't quick enough to make his escape, Helmut would give him the pummeling of his life, always protected by his story of the assaulted woman.

Helmut's super*macho* image, bolstered by his "Mr. Clean" pose, was a transparent cover-up for his latent homosexuality. Not that Helmut let himself so much as suspect such a possibility. He hated gays. Whenever he was at a male porno film and "one of those queers" sat next to him, Helmut pushed him away fast, with a threat of beating him to a pulp.

"Porno films?" I inquired. "Helmut, what are you doing at male porno films?" Immediately, Helmut became defensive. "What do you think I'm doing there? I'm checking out physiques. The guys in those films keep in shape, you know. Say, are you insinuating I go there to watch that disgusting filth?"

Certainly not, Helmut! Who would ever suspect a

tough muscleman like you of wanting to watch two
males having sex? A virile man like you who restricts
himself to intercourse with his wife once a month because he's saving his strength?

The Helmuts of this world have a formidable problem. They're caught between Scylla and Charybdis, and
so are the therapists who try to help them. Neither their
real selves nor their images are able to satisfy them, and
the two are so distanced from each other that a compromise isn't possible. Helmut would have been better
off if we had been able to talk about his homosexual
feelings, but he was so shut off from himself, he wasn't
aware he had any.

A BREAK IN ROUTINE

By trusting the real you when it suggests imposing some
limitations, you'll become stronger, not weaker as you
fear. You'll stop draining yourself, and when you do
participate in an event, you'll have something real to
offer. Give your image permission to rest awhile and
stop being buffeted about by what people will think.
Don't feel you have to be the life of every party or
Johnny-on-the-spot for that backbreaking assignment.
And if people tease you or ask what's wrong, try taking
a deep breath and saying, "I just don't feel up to it."
That won't be easy for your proud-spirited image to go
along with, but if you can accomplish it, congratulate
yourself. You've taken a big step in the right direction.

Perhaps, like George, part of the reason your energy
is diminishing is that you're not sleeping well at night.
Not just occasionally when you've had too much coffee
or become keyed up about something special. But most
nights. That kind of sleeplessness is usually rooted in
tension and stress, and before you turn to sleeping pills,
which was what George had been doing, try some measures that will dispel the symptoms instead of masking
them.

One very positive step you can take is to break your patterns. If your work is extremely structured—if you're an architect, for example, who spends all day doing precise renderings—start drawing again in the evenings . . . or finger painting . . . or modeling clay. Anything that can be as sloppy and formless as you wish. You'll probably be getting back to something you once enjoyed, and you'll be giving yourself a much-needed diversion.

Work with figures all day? Try crossword puzzles or detective stories. Exercise your brain in a different way. Take up the guitar or the piano if you sit at meetings all day listening to people talk. Your ears will welcome a new kind of sound. Pick whatever it is you think you'll enjoy—as long as it's not the same as what you've been concentrating on for so long. I've found that mothers who are beginning to burn out are often thrilled by taking a course in a subject they've always wanted to learn. For a little while each week, they reverse their role: Instead of being teacher all the time, they can be student. They can ask questions and expect answers. And they make quiet time for themselves so that they can prepare their assignments.

THE HIGH COST OF ASPIRATIONS

People who set high goals for themselves seem to have a built-in need for recognition. As long as their efforts are paying off, their energy continues to flow. But as soon as life settles into a routine pattern, an uncomfortable listlessness overtakes them. They no longer feel rooted or involved, even in situations that were so vital to them before. Sometimes this is brought about by unrealized goals, but more often it is a result of unrealistic expectations. When people paint grandiose pictures for themselves of what it's going to be like on the next plateau, more often than not what they've envisioned doesn't materialize. Not because they don't reach the plateau. They do. But once they're there, the scenery isn't too different from the scenery lower down, and disenchantment begins to set in.

Miriam's Story

Miriam had dreamed all her life of becoming an actress. Way back, when visitors asked that cliché question, "What do you want to be when you grow up?" she answered, "An actress, of course." Everyone thought, "How cute!" and paid no attention. But Miriam was serious. She was always getting her friends involved in putting on a play. She tried out for everything in school, and if she didn't land a part, she helped with costumes or scenery or anything that was needed. Whenever she could, she went to the theater, and she constantly borrowed books of plays from the library.

When it was time for college, Miriam chose one that was famous for its drama department. She was excited to be studying with professionals, and she worked harder than ever. No matter how hard she worked, though, she was never tired. She had plenty of energy for her drama activities, her other studies, and a busy social life. Miriam was popular. No one who knew her in those years doubted that she'd be a success.

The next step on Miriam's agenda was New York and the heart of the theater world, neither of which, she soon found out, had exactly been waiting for her. It isn't necessary to chronicle all the setbacks and disappointments she went through. They were numerous and typical. But Miriam took them in stride. When she couldn't find theater work, she did the usual—waited on tables to make enough money to cover her rent and lessons and carfare to auditions. When she landed a bit part or an appearance in a commercial, she plunged into it enthusiastically, each time convinced this would be the one. Throughout these years, Miriam was happy. She had friends and dates and, above all, she had her dream.

Little by little, that dream began to come true. Miriam got good notices in a small part, and her career took off. A few seasons later, she was offered a starring role in a Broadway production. Wow! This was it! What she had hoped for all her life.

Rehearsals were difficult—repetitious and tiring. Lines were rewritten and had to be relearned. There were flare-ups and quarrels and dissension among various members of the cast. Through it all, Miriam stayed calm. She never lost her temper or her patience. And gradually, her spirit prevailed. The play began to take shape; the cast became a cohesive group. They opened to rave reviews.

"I'll never forget that opening night," Miriam told me. "If there really is such a thing as a peak experience, that was it. Everyone I knew was in the audience. My family. Friends from school. New York buddies. Everyone. There was electricity in the air, and I knew—even before we went on—it was going to be a smash."

While Miriam described that night she was so animated and radiant I couldn't imagine what she was doing in my office. But finally, the description of the night ended, and as she went on talking, I could see and hear the animation fade. It was as if she were acting out a Burn-Out for me. Her face looked drawn, and her voice sounded expressionless. "It's everything I ever wanted," she said. "I lived on that high for days. But now I want to quit. I have trouble making myself go to the theater every evening. I'm tired all the time. I'm not even acting well."

At first, it was difficult to see what had happened to Miriam. Her story didn't offer much in the way of clues. I started to probe for possible causes—a disappointing romance, disapproval from someone she respected. I looked for deep-rooted behavior patterns she might be re-enacting. Finally, however, it became clear that Miriam was showing signs of a Burn-Out. While she was still a youngster, she had dedicated and committed herself to becoming a star, and she had conjured up her own vision of what a star's life was like. In her child's mind, of course, it would be something like Cinderella—drudgery and hard work for years, then one day, a magic wand, beautiful clothes, elegant balls, a coach and four horses, a handsome prince. If you remember that Burn-Out is inevitable "whenever the expectation level is dramatically opposed to reality and the person persists in trying to reach that expectation," you'll find it easy to see what Miriam had done to herself. While she seemed to have reached her expectation when she achieved stardom, she hadn't really, because to her, being a star was something quite different from what it turned out to be.

Opening night was really closing night for Miriam. It had been the culmination of her lifetime. She had been the recipient of accolades and admiration. She had felt powerful. But where was all that hoopla the next day? Oh sure, the audience applauded, but that was about it. Her name wasn't in the papers. Her relatives weren't flying in to compliment her. No prince was pursuing her with a glass slipper in his hand. Her triumph had turned into a routine. Her starring part was just another job!

And that is one of the high costs of aspiration: The payoff seldom seems commensurate with either the dream or the effort spent. And yet if Miriam had never made it, she would always have imagined how wonderful it would have been. Because of her particular personality, either circumstance could have led her to Burn-Out. As Oscar Wilde put it, "In this world there are two tragedies. One is not getting what one wants, the other is getting it."

CHECKING YOUR FEELINGS

Do you see any parallels between yourself and Miriam? Have you ever felt that severe letdown after the exhilaration of achieving some goal? Think of your high-school or college graduation. Your wedding. The birth of your first baby. Your last promotion. What happened afterward? Once the initial high was over, did your energy seem to drain away, leaving you listless and depressed? Did you find yourself feeling detached from your accomplishment—standing outside it, so to speak? Were you suddenly responding cynically to praise or interested questions?

All these—tiredness, detachment, cynicism—are Burn-Out symptoms. They are uncomfortable feeling states which indicate that in some way you have depleted your resources and your ability to function. They are also the precursors of other uncomfortable feelings, so it's important not to let them go unchecked. Had Miriam not come for help as soon as she did, she might have destroyed her career with her first starring role. One of two things would have happened. Either she'd have been overcome by her disappointment and quit, which was what she told me she wanted to do, or she'd have suppressed her feelings and forced herself to work harder and harder in search of some gratification. The first possibility isn't too likely, since the Miriams of this world don't quit so easily. What they're much more apt to do is deplete themselves in a struggle to deny that anything is wrong. For some people. That works for a while, but for Miriam, who was constantly in the spotlight, the pretense would have been unmasked in short order, and audiences would have been put off by what they'd have perceived as a lack of sincerity.

If you've been involved in this kind of attempt to disguise a disappointing situation or relationship, you know it's a losing battle. Denial, as we'll see later on, is a voracious drainer of energy, and as your energy ebbs, Burn-Out becomes self-generating. One symptom leads to the next until it seems nothing short of the cavalry will be able to rescue you. Your world begins to shrink. Pretty soon, you're putting everything you have left into the one particular situation which you consider to be the focal point of your life, letting every other area go. If it's the job that's the source of your discomfort, you stay later and take more work home, so you have no time for the activities that once refreshed you. If you've become a tennis nut and that begins to fail you, you go at it with such a vengeance you conk out the minute you get off the court. If you've been devoting yourself to a sick or difficult child who doesn't seem to be responding, you renew your efforts until you end up neglecting your marriage and your other children.

Whenever efforts are disproportionate to the result they're producing, something is sorely amiss. It's one thing to work harder and get a situation straightened out, whether it's on the job or with your child. It's fine to practice through a tennis slump until you see yourself making progress. But becoming totally bogged down in a situation that's going nowhere is an entirely different matter. It's an exercise in avoidance, signifying that an individual is fleeing from the real issue—namely, that something is inherently wrong with the circumstances. Either they were never right to begin with or they have become unsatisfying along the way.

Often in the course of a lifetime, it becomes necessary to review our choices and to admit that a goal or a career or a relationship was a mistake. People who are able to sit down and do this with some degree of objectivity open themselves up to options and solutions. They can decide either to forego some of their idealized standards and be contented with a compromise or to abandon the situation entirely and go on to something else. Unfortunately, some people can't do this, and they're our Burn-Out types. They have brought their habitual dedication and commitment to some thankless situation, and they find it virtually impossible to let go. They're imbued with the notion that a little more effort, a little more insight will turn the trick. Admitting defeat is simply not within their frame of reference, and so they wear themselves out trying to make an impossible situation work or trying to invest a meaningless relationship with meaning.

This kind of perseverance is admirable in a way. It's part of the behavior pattern that made our Burn-Out successful in the first place. Only here it is misapplied and signifies that the person is stuck in making himself, rather than the situation, right. His actions have become ends in and of themselves rather than means to effect some change. By generating so much activity, he has detached himself from the actual problem and the necessity to face what he perceives deep down as his own weakness. In his book, problems are acceptable; weakness isn't.

One of the surest ways to ascertain whether our efforts have become disproportionate to the circumstances is to listen to the people who care about us. If we're always getting comments like, "Why don't you give yourself a break?" the chances are we should. Other people are noticing how futilely we're knocking ourselves out. Why aren't we? We're certainly perceptive enough about what the next guy is doing. We see at a glance when a relative or friend is stuck in a hopeless situation or is perpetuating an empty relationship. We recognize instantly the couple (like Philip and Doris) who is so into "intimacy and joy" that it has to be fake. Words like "sweetheart" and "dear" often pepper their conversation, and they're always talking about each other in glowing terms. But the voices belie the words. We hear no sound of enthusiasm or genuine feeling in what they're saying, nor do we catch any glimpses of affection in the way they behave toward each other. The relationship has become rote and routine, even distant.

Think about the situations in your life and how they make you feel. Concentrate particularly on three areas: Do these situations supply you with energy or drain you? Do you feel involved in them or detached? Are you enthusiastic about them or cynical?

Jot down your answers and then describe the way you *feel* about your *feelings*. Keep in mind that one symptom leads to another. For instance, if you're feeling exhausted, are you angry about it? If you're detached, does that depress you? If you're cynical, are you also experiencing disappointment in your surroundings?

Keep your notes. They'll be a helpful checklist as we look further into the feeling state of Burn-Out. A feeling recognized and explained can quickly fade away, as it did for Miriam when she realized how strongly she felt cheated and why.

"THEY'RE DOING THIS TO ME"

Miriam had been hard hit by the disappointing difference between the dream and the reality, yet she had been unable to pinpoint what was bothering her. She had vague feelings of disappointment and anger, but the closest she could come to expressing her feelings when she sat down to talk to me was, "It was supposed to be different." Where, specifically, had she gotten that supposition? She didn't know, but the clue to her problem seemed to lie in those six words. We pursued the thought until Miriam was able to take it one step further and admit to me that she felt as if she had been cheated. "By whom?" I asked. She wasn't sure. "Just cheated," she said. "As if somebody let me down." When I asked Miriam if she thought her parents had been the culprits, she was quick to answer, "No. In fact, they did their best to discourage me. They thought anything would be better than acting. The whole thing was my idea. I really can't blame anyone else."

Perhaps the same is true of you. You take full responsibility for your choices. You seem always to have known what you wanted to be, and you were happy to go about being it. Nothing could have deterred you from becoming the world's greatest teacher or the best mother on the block or a career woman or a writer or a very rich person. Well, now that you've reached your goal and you're finding it less than satisfactory, you may be wondering if you have to add to your feelings of Burn-Out by accepting all that blame. The answer is an emphatic, "No, you don't."

Even if there's no one specific at whom you can point a finger and say, "It was all your fault," a lot of what has been going wrong can be attributed to the permissive condition of the world around us. Like Peter Pan, we are living in Never-Never Land, and as I have mentioned before, much of the blame can be ascribed to the times we live in.

Years ago, when religion was flourishing and the Puritan ethic was in force, we relied on God and our earthly circumstances to set limits for us. We worked hard and were glad of the opportunity to do it. Our jobs were means of subsistence, not self-aggrandizement. If we enjoyed them, fine. If we didn't, we were still happy to be earning a living. The same thing with our marriages. We didn't expect them to be as romantic as Gothic novels, so we were not quite so disappointed with our humdrum existences. We stayed close to our families and were content with simple pleasures. Since we knew everyone in town and everyone in town knew us, it was important not to flout the conventions because at the least we'd be talked about; in the extreme, we'd be ostracized.

None of this is to suggest that life was "better" then or that people didn't have problems. It's just that the problems were different and certainly not of the nature of Burn-Out. Burn-Out doesn't stem from too few expectations, but from too many. And over the years, our world—particularly in America—has become a storehouse of expectations. Every day, in a thousand ways, the world sends us messages that life *can* be beautiful. When we go off to college, it tells us, we will have the freedom to make decisions with no parental interference. Only someone forgot to add that experience is a great help in making decisions, and so far we've had no experience. Many promising students burn out before graduation because after they get into the college of their choice it bears no relationship to what they thought they were choosing. It may be large and impersonal, or class-conscious, or a round of burdensome work that doesn't seem relevant to the future.

Often it does turn out to have been irrelevant. When the young student leaves the campus and joins the work force, he finds a far different world from the one he was led to expect. Textbooks are one thing; actual working conditions are another. Sitting in a library, studying procedures, our student sees a job as a logical series of steps leading to a logical conclusion. When he ventures into the business world, he finds all manner of stumbling blocks and detours he hadn't counted on. It's something like planning a conversation in advance. You know just how it's going to go: You'll say X, then the other person will say Y, and in no time, you'll arrive at Z. Only when you get started, the other person says B . . . and you're thrown off base.

In every field, there is such a discrepancy between the world of academe and what's really out there it's no wonder young people see their expectations crumble. The budding advertising writer who thinks life is going to be a round of clever headlines and descriptive copy adding up to a tasteful, but persuasive, ad is in for a rude shock when the client wants to say, "15¢ Off. Buy now." The young lawyer who expects a precise world of theory and clear-cut precedents finds himself coping with shortcuts and expedients that were not in any legal textbook. He also finds himself dealing with confused, angry clients who want results and are not particularly interested in the ramifications of the law.

Just recently I chatted with a newly graduated architect who had spent his last five years struggling with designs and plans and artistic conceptions. He had been indoctrinated with the principle that the architect's responsibility is to impart beauty and individuality to the world around us. In his courses, months were allotted for every design assignment; multiple solutions were worked out for every problem. Imagine his letdown when he started his first job and found buildings being designed, not in months, but in minutes. Costs, not aesthetics, were now the underlying considerations, and time was money as surely as bricks and mortar. If my young friend is planning to succeed in his career, he'll have to do a lot of accommodating between his principles and the realities.

The same thing happens in later life. We go to the movies and see that when we reach the executive suite, we'll have carpeted offices and expense accounts and power. Very seldom does anyone remind us of the endless, dull meetings, the dreary reports, the office politics with all the lying, treachery, back-stabbing, and in-fighting. Women read in trendy magazines of being "liberated" and taking charge of their lives, but the articles make light of the struggle to pay the rent, the countless evenings spent alone, or the demands made on women by men who have also read the articles.

Coming to the big city and embarking on a career *can* be exciting, but with one's family thousands of miles away and one's support system essentially absent, a lot of unexpected disappointments can crop up. And even if they don't, the satisfactions often aren't what they were cracked up to be. So we turn to the "trappings," the material possessions the media tell us will make us feel good: the jazzy car, the ten-room house, the swimming pool, the designer wardrobe. We place a lot of emphasis on the external manifestations of success, and we grow away from ourselves. When we have a disappointment, we "treat ourselves" to some extravagance until our feelings become repressed and the goods become ends in and of themselves.

Some of us turn to experiences—extramarital affairs, kinky sex, a little cocaine, skydiving. As we'll see later, in the chapter "False Cures," any one of these pursuits can—does—supply momentary excitement, but none of them has any substance, and we find ourselves doing more and more bizarre things to bring on new highs. Since life bears a great resemblance to a teeter-totter, up one minute, down the next, this means our valleys become deeper in severity, and we pay an ever-higher price for our peak experiences.

The Nonfeeling State of Burn-Out

❧

So far, in the realm of Burn-Out feelings, we've touched on loss of energy, detachment, and cynicism. It's easy to see how my young architect friend, after a sheltered childhood in an affluent suburb, rounded off by five years in a university, could eventually burn out in his work situation, either by becoming cynical about it or detached from it. A lot depends on how strongly he has pinned his hopes on his profession and how secure he is within himself. If he needs the job for his own feelings of self-worth and doesn't have much in the way of outside resources, he may find himself rushing pell-mell into Burn-Out. If, on the other hand, he's fortunate enough to adjust his experiences and guide himself away from the pitfalls, he can make peace with his carer and reap rewards from it.

One of the ways to check Burn-Out at or before its onset is to know what symptoms to look for, so if you get out the jottings you made in the preceding chapter, we'll look at all the possible symptoms one by one, and you can see which of them apply to you.

EXHAUSTION

Loss of energy and the accompanying feelings of weariness are usually the first distress signals. Exhaustion is hard for the potential Burn-Out to face because it's a complete reversal from the high energy level he's accustomed to and relies on for keeping up with his crowded schedule. Pay special attention to tiredness. It's the best indicator for catching Burn-Out early, and although it's hard to face, it's easy to recognize. If you've been having trouble keeping up with your usual round of activities, don't fall into the trap of pushing yourself harder. And don't panic. You'll just be making matters worse. Instead, acknowledge how tired you feel and don't make any excuses for it. It's probably not permanent. It doesn't even have to be long-range, as long as you don't take the wrong steps and exacerbate the problem.

DETACHMENT

Detachment begins as a self-protective device to help ward off pain. When you feel let down by people and situations, there's a temptation to tell yourself, "I don't care, it wasn't important anyway," and move away from the things that used to involve you. When you separate yourself from people and events, you strip them of their power to hurt you. Unfortunately, you also diminish their power to affect you in positive ways, and detachment has a way of intensifying into the more serious D's—Disengagement, Distancing, Dulling, and Deadness.

BOREDOM AND CYNICISM

These are natural companions—one begets the other; detachment begets them both. Once you're on the periphery of the world around you instead of deep in the center of it, it's hard to remain interested in what's going on. You begin to question the value of activities and friendships, even of life itself. You become skeptical of people's motives and blasé about causes.

IMPATIENCE AND HEIGHTENED IRRITABILITY

While these are very similar, impatience in a mild form is a built-in characteristic of Burn-Out candidates. With their vast supply of energy, they have always been able to do things quickly and get on to something else, a quality which never tended to make them overly sympathetic to the plodder. As the Burn-Out increases and their own ability to accomplish things diminishes, their impatience grows and spills over into irritability with everyone around them. Flare-ups occur that seem totally out of character as the Burn-Out blames his family and co-workers for things that were more his fault than theirs.

A SENSE OF OMNIPOTENCE

This is the symptom that came through so clearly in George's case. "No one else can do it. Only I can." Sentiments like that are not the expression of a healthy ego. They're an exaggeration bordering on the delusional. Be assured—somebody else can do it. Maybe not the same way you'd have done it or with the same degree of excellence, but it may be a situation that doesn't require excellence. A person who feels he's indispensable is in reality a block to progress and the initiative of others.

A SUSPICION OF BEING UNAPPRECIATED

With the decrease in energy comes an increase of effort, but not necessarily of result. The Burn-Out, of course, never sees that, and he feels aggrieved at the lack of appreciation people are showing toward him. After all, they're leaving early; he's staying late. The least they could do is say, "Thank you." He gets bitter and increasingly angry.

PARANOIA

It's just one small step from feeling unappreciated to feeling downright mistreated. When things are going wrong, as we saw with Miriam, a vague feeling sets in that *someone* must be at fault. In Miriam's case, there was no specific villain she could point to, but as Burn-Out advances, a target is usually found. The boss, co-workers, a spouse, a child—anyone handy will serve. What's constant in a paranoid condition is that the Burn-Out feels put upon, mistreated, and increasingly suspicious of his environment and the people around him, possibly even members of his family.

DISORIENTATION

As a Burn-Out advances, the individual feels a growing separation from his environment. Somehow, something is just a little out of kilter. Things are happening that he doesn't quite understand. He sits at a meeting or social situation, his thoughts a thousand miles away, then suddenly realizes he can't recall a word of what Smith just said. Since the Burn-Out already suspects his competence is slipping away, this kind of episode heightens his sense of agitation. It also heightens his paranoia. He will wonder—at best—whether Smith had noticed his lack of attention; at worst—whether Smith had been talking about him.

I'd like to expand on this feeling of disorientation a little, because it can be a serious source of disturbance, creating a cycle of more agitation and more disorientation. A person who is burning out will have difficulty with his thought processes. His cognitive powers will suffer, not from "old age" or "senility," as he may jokingly remark, but from the agitation he's creating inside himself. His speech patterns will falter as he finds himself forgetting what he started to say. Names and dates will elude him. His concentration span will be much more limited.

Naturally, this is very upsetting since it affects one's perceptions, judgment, and ability to make decisions. It may lead to unfair treatment of other people or faulty problem-solving. But if something of this sort is happening to you, be sure to realize you're not losing your faculties. You're fatigued, and your system is overloaded. Actually, you can check this for yourself by noticing where it is you're not functioning. Observe whether it's only in specific areas. For instance, are you perfectly able to do a puzzle or the children's math homework and yet continue to be stymied at work? If so, try to plan for some time off. Even a long weekend may go far toward helping you break the cycle of disorientation and agitation.

PSYCHOSOMATIC COMPLAINTS

That phrase is very often misunderstood, so it's important to clarify what we mean by it here. In no way are we using it to designate malingering or to imply that the sufferer isn't actually feeling ill. Psychosomatic complaints are real, but they're induced or prolonged by stress and emotional tension. They have as much of the psychological as the physical about them. Headaches, colds that linger, backaches—all these are signs that something is wrong, and it's usually something the person doesn't want to look at. Somehow, physical complaints seem more "respectable" than emotional ones, and easier to cope with. So we avoid facing what's going on inside us and "have a cold." Psychosomatic complaints are often early signs of Burn-Out.

DEPRESSION

Depression can take many forms and may or may not be connected to a Burn-Out. There are differences between a generally depressed state of mind and the form of depression which signifies that a Burn-Out is taking place. In a nonrelated depression, the condition is prolonged and pervades all areas of a person's life. He may sit staring into space, or he may sleep for much of the day. He may lose his appetite for food and his desire for sex. Life will seem meaningless to such a person, and he may even become suicidal. In a Burn-Out, however, the depression is usually temporary, specific, and localized, pertaining more or less to one area of life. For instance, a Burn-Out can be despondent and downcast on the job, but go home and play tennis. A depressed person can't make such separations. A general lethargy pervades all his activities. There is another distinction: the presence of guilt. Whereas the depressed person is likely to feel a profound guilt for everything that's going wrong, the Burn-Out is more apt to be angry.

That's a long list, and possibly a scary one, so let me reassure you before we go any further. Even if you nodded your head "yes" to every single one of those symptoms, don't be alarmed. It probably means only that you're tense and tired and tending to exaggerate your situation. Also, there are degrees to everything, and you may be experiencing nothing more severe than the early stages of any given item. Besides, a symptom is not a disease. It's simply one part of an alert system that's telling you something's amiss and it's time to take action. If you think of those Burn-Out symptoms the way you would think of a sneeze, you can put them to good use. When you suddenly start sneezing, what goes through your mind? Not whether the sneeze was loud or soft or single or part of a series, but what does it signify? Are you developing an allergy? Getting a cold? Or did someone just dump the pepper can?

If you do the same thing with your Burn-Out symptoms, they can lead you back into positive directions. When you notice yourself feeling bored, don't just yawn and walk away. Ask yourself what's behind that boredom: Is there someone in the room you don't like? Are you detaching yourself from the situation because you're angry? Pay attention to your feelings and let them guide you toward a deeper look at yourself. It may be uncomfortable, but as long as you're allowing yourself to feel, you're in a good place, willing to face up to your problems and make some changes.

The real danger in a Burn-Out situation is *nonfeeling,* the denial that anything is wrong. As soon as denial enters the picture, the person's symptoms become enemies instead of allies. They're no longer able to help, because no matter how loudly they cry out, no one is listening. Denial heralds a second stage of Burn-Out, just as exhaustion heralds the first, so it's important for us to look at denial in some depth. Before we do, however, it's a good idea for you to see if denial is creeping into your behavior. Do this simple check. Ask yourself how many times lately you've caught yourself saying, or thinking, "I don't care." Then ask yourself if it's true that underneath all those protective layers you've built up there's no caring left.

DENIAL OF FEELINGS

Since we know that people who are subject to Burn-Out are the carers among us, it doesn't make sense to assume that one day, for no particular reason, the caring simply stopped, even though many Burn-Outs will insist that this is so. Far more logical is the assumption that the caring has been shut off for a very good reason—and shut off by the person himself. In every case of Burn-Out I've treated, if the individual can be induced to look hard enough and long enough, he eventually uncovers the "disappearance trail."

Martha's Story

Martha, an attractive woman in her early thirties, came to see me because she had decided to leave her husband and child and wanted an opinion as to whether her leaving would have a harmful effect on her six-year-old daughter. Now, that's a pretty dramatic step for a young woman to take, and you'd expect someone about to take it to be in a rather agitated state. Not Martha. In fact, she was so far from being emotional—so cool, so detached from her problem that she didn't even tell me what she had come to see me about. If I had been asked to guess, I might have said, "She must need advice for a relative." Even when she called for an appointment, I was struck by her calm, efficient approach. "Is this Dr. Freudenberger? If it's possible, I'd like to see you for an hour this week. Would Thursday at one be convenient?" It sounded as if she had me confused with the local hairdresser, and I had to resist the impulse to ask if she wanted a manicure or just a haircut!

Now keep in mind as you read on that I've told *you* why Martha was there, but Martha hadn't told me! When she arrived on Friday at three, her hair looked great and so did she. She greeted me and got right to what I thought was the point. "I'm planning to go to the West Coast, and it would be very inconvenient to take Ellen along. Would my absence be traumatic to a child her age? She's very fond of her father."

Since my own high standards come into play once in a while, I feel forced to admit that I didn't begin to get what she was really about to do. I thought she was going away for a week or two and was being overprotective. I asked some questions about Ellen: Was she outgoing? Did she have playmates? Was she unusually attached to Martha? When I was satisfied that Ellen

was a pretty typical, normal six-year-old, I said, "I'm
sure you can go and enjoy yourself. Ellen will be just
fine until you get back." Martha looked at me in aston-
ishment. "But that's just it, Doctor. I'm not coming
back."

I must have been silent longer than I realized because Martha stood up to go. In the same unruffled
way she had talked to me on the telephone, she asked
what she owed me. "An explanation," I answered, in a
much gruffer tone than I had used before. It took some
doing, but I finally got Martha to sit down and tell me
the real issue. In answer to my questions, she explained
that she was going off with a young man (a boy,
really). He was ten years younger than she, hadn't
"found" himself as yet, but was sure he'd do better in
California. How had she met him? He had worked at
her local garage that summer. How would they live?
She was sure she could get work. She used to have a
responsible job.

Martha gave me all these answers in a polite, expressionless voice. She might have been talking to a census
taker. Even when I asked about her husband, I could
sense no emotion. Nothing was wrong between them. It
was just that she had fallen in love with someone else. I
knew there would be no point in trying to get her to see
that something *had* to be wrong, that she couldn't possibly have fallen in love with the young man she had described to me, or that she didn't even sound like a
woman in love, so I played for time by expressing some
concern about Ellen now that I knew Martha was leaving for good. I brought up some practical matters I
thought she ought to settle before she left, and in that
way I got her to make another appointment.

Martha was so out of touch with her feelings that she
had trouble admitting she really didn't want to go off
with her young lover even though I was able to detain
her after every visit. As soon as I would suggest that
she postpone leaving for another few days, she would
agree. Finally, I felt I had enough background data and
enough of Martha's trust to allow us to get down to
business. I had noticed during our few talks that, even

as a child, Martha had always been obedient and done what was expected of her. Once or twice when I questioned a particular episode, she shrugged and said, "Oh I didn't mind. It was okay with me." I had also noticed that she had referred to her "responsible job" more than once, although she had never gone into detail about it.

I suspected the job would be a good starting point, and it turned out to be. Together, Martha and I uncovered years of repressed resentment that had begun to accumulate when her husband expected her to stop working and stay home with Ellen. As much as Martha had loved her job and her image of herself as a career woman headed for important things, she wanted to do the "right" thing for her child. Well, according to her early training and her husband, the "right" thing was to be a full-time mother, so Martha denied her feelings and agreed. She not only said nothing to her husband about the way she felt, she didn't allow herself to think about it. She fell right into her new routine with the same dedication she had brought to her job and went about being a good wife and mother with determination.

Over the years, Martha had grown more and more phlegmatic. When I asked why she hadn't brought up the subject of work again as Ellen got older, she shrugged and said it no longer seemed to matter. According to Martha, nothing much mattered—at least in the early stages of our work together. But the real tipoff to how sad her life had become came when I asked her what had drawn her to her young man. "He makes me laugh," she said.

Martha exemplifies clearly what I referred to before as the dangerous progression of Denial: those insidious four D's—Disengagement, Distancing, Dulling, and Deadness. From the time she had denied her intense desire to work and be successful in her own right, Martha had become increasingly distant from herself and her surroundings. She went around in an emotional stupor, going through the motions but not allowing herself to be affected. Fortunately, she was bright and was able, in a relatively short time, to see what she had been doing, how she had latched onto the lover as one more substitute for facing the real issue. With the help of her husband, who admitted that he, too, had been guilty of denial, we were able to get Martha and the marriage back on track. Today she's working, Ellen's happy with school and a sitter while her mother is gone, and Martha's husband has his old, vivacious wife back.

WHY WE DENY

Essentially, the willingness and ability to feel are what give meaning to life. If we didn't feel or care, we wouldn't strive or love or build cathedrals or create civilizations. No matter how scientific or seemingly intellectual an endeavor is, some emotion initially impelled the doer to undertake it. It might have been anything from curiosity to ambition, altruism to greed, but it *was* an emotion. As long as we stay in touch with our feelings, we're alive and vital and engaged in life. And I'm not talking just about the "good" feelings. Of course, it's great to be experiencing love or joy, but even anger or sorrow is preferable to a void.

If you've gone through even a brief period of nonfeeling like Martha's, you know that at such times the world takes on the aspects of a bad play. You're aware that something's going on, but you're not caught up in it. What participation you do muster is halfhearted and surface deep, without spirit or interest. No matter how frantically you plunge yourself into activities (and we'll have a lot to say about that later), you derive no satisfaction. Why then, do people deny?

Obviously, as we all know from our own experiences, feelings can be painful. When we care a lot or love intensely, we give situations and people power over us. Often they let us down, wound us, even desert us. And because we care, we're vulnerable. We've opened ourselves up to disappointment and hurt. The obvious answer to this vulnerability is *not* to care, *not* to let anyone get inside our defenses, *not* to place importance on any external circumstances. "If I get the promotion, fine. If I don't, who cares? It would probably have meant a lot of extra work."

Sometimes this denial or distancing of feelings can be traced all the way back to childhood. There are families who teach their children not to feel. Those messages, again. "Don't be so emotional." "Why don't you think instead of rushing into things?" "Look at Mary. She's crying at that silly program."

The "don't feel" message can be transmitted in many ways. Some parents are totally incapable of expressing warmth and affection. Others may verbalize love in a formal way, but never hug or kiss or touch. In some families, the only emotion ever expressed is anger; that's the only way contact is made, and the child gets the impression that all emotions are frightening. Children from homes like these learn to repress their feelings at an early age. Their adjustment to the world becomes almost totally cerebral: They learn to approach and respond to pleasures intellectually rather than emotionally. Somewhere, way deep down, their emotions are still in operation, but the person has so distanced himself from them that their effect is never felt.

Not all denial dates back so far. Sometimes it starts after a great hurt—the loss of a loved one, the death of someone close, or a grave disappointment in something sought after. Or, as is very common in Burn-Out, it can be a recent condition which has built up gradually as a protection from the less severe, but more constant, frustrations of unrealized hopes. To guard against further disappointments, the person falls into the habit of standing apart from situations and merely acting out a role in them. Martha is really an embodiment of all three of these circumstances. She *had* been taught to control her emotions as a child, but she had merely restrained, not repressed them. Then, when she had to forego her career, she bottled herself up further, becoming "deader and deader" as her frustration grew.

"FOR GOD'S SAKE, DON'T BE LIKE . . ."

One of the most harmful messages a family can give a child is the negative one not to be like somebody. "Whatever you do, don't be like Uncle Charlie, that no-good bastard." "Oh, there you go, sounding like Aunt Bess again." In some families it's the father who's the bad example. Maybe he never earned a decent living or lived up to his wife's expectations, and the children are not allowed to forget it. If we go back to George for a minute, we can see how this can affect an entire life by leading to denial.

While George and I were tracing some of his patterns back to his childhood, I asked him many times about his father, but George never had much to say. His father was no more than a shadowy figure in his memory, and we always ended up discussing his mother. She was vivid to George. According to him, she had always kept the house neat, cooked marvelous meals, helped with homework, and been a virtual saint. "Did she spend a lot of time with your father?" I asked one day. No hesitation this time. "Oh they didn't have much in common. And besides, she had too much to do, because he never earned enough for her to have help."

Aha! So that's where George's compulsion had begun. *His* wife would have help. George would see to that. And *his* wife would never be able to complain that he didn't earn enough. That first remark opened up the floodgates for George, and a lot of memories of his father came rushing back. A lot of memories of quarrels, too. George was amazed that he had forgotten all those quarrels, but now as he relived them, he realized how his mother's scathing tones and his father's constant apologies had set him firmly on his workaholic course.

What George had been denying all his adult life was that he could be even remotely like his father and therefore a failure. But one of the prices we all pay for denial is that along with the bad, we deny the good.

Over the years, George had orphaned himself by blotting out all his pictures of his father and allowing them to be superseded by his mother's one-sided, negative portrait. Now he saw that he had unwittingly deprived himself of his father's gentleness and compassion.

What makes that message, "Don't be like . . ." so detrimental is that, because it's nonselective, it robs you of your power to pick and choose. It doesn't say, "Don't be a failure, but *do* be compassionate and gentle." It says, in essence, "Dismiss that person," and so turns into a case of throwing out the baby with the bath water. Since you've been instructed categorically to distance yourself from the person, you must also distance yourself from any positive modeling he might have been able to offer you. You have to block out large chunks of your past, and in George's case this meant forgetting all the instances of fun he had had with his father and all the times his father had been a source of comfort to him. His mother's message, which he obeyed more comprehensively than she had probably intended, turned out to be a very costly one. In the process of escaping his father's failure pattern in financial matters, George forfeited many loving traits. He became so thoroughly *not like* his father that he never took time to have fun with his children or listen to their problems. Nor was he the kind of faithful, supportive husband his father had been. The "Don't be like . . ." had prevailed in many damaging ways, as George's Burn-Out testified.

THE MANY FORMS OF DENIAL

Denial of Failure. In George, we see a specific instance of the fear of failure and the circumstances that led him first to denial and then to Burn-Out. Obviously, no two instances of any problem are precisely alike, but failure is a widespread fear in our world today, and in almost all cases, the way we live has a lot to do with promoting it. It used to be, if you were going through hard times, someone in the family would take you in or at least "tide you over." The neighborhood grocer would extend you credit. Now we've become so spread out that our families are often hundreds of miles away, and our friendly corner grocery store has metamorphosed into the impersonal supermarket.

We have no provisions for failure at the very time when taxes, inflation, and the emphasis on material comforts are making it more difficult to manage. This, necessarily, intensifies our anxiety and puts us into a position of constant stress. As our country became more and more affluent, we all began to take a comfortable life for granted. A home with our own backyard; one car certainly, but more than likely, two; color TV; good schools for the children. The time for saving was always tomorrow. Today, there was one more thing to buy. It's very easy to fall into the "good" life, but not so easy to relinquish it if things go wrong. The luxury you decide to treat yourself to in a weak moment becomes a necessity very quickly. For the wage earner, traditionally the man, there's an ongoing fear of not being able to maintain his and his family's "necessities." Until recently, women were more or less exempted from this kind of fear. True, as in Nancy's case, they were sometimes expected to excel in certain skills or roles, but these rarely extended to earning a living and supporting a family. Now, however, with the new freedoms and the increasing divorce rate, women are subject to the same pressures as men, and the denial of failure has become a very real factor in their lives.

For Burn-Out candidates, moreover, there is still another dimension to their struggle against failure, and that is the often unrealistic standards they set for themselves. Success is a very personal affair. To one man, twenty thousand dollars a year may represent more than he ever dreamed of. He may come home nightly to his modest home and feel that he's in a castle. He's content with his accomplishments, and therefore he thinks of himself, rightly, as a success. To another man, fifty thousand dollars or a hundred thousand dollars may be less than he expected of himself, and if it is, he'll think of himself as a failure. No matter that the world admires him and considers him a man of accomplishment. In his mind, he has fallen short, and if he's troubled enough, he may be driven to deny his imagined failure by overextending himself financially or bolstering his ego with extramarital affairs. Unless he can come to terms with who he is and what he has achieved, he will be an unhappy human being in constant need of proving something to himself.

Denial of Fear. Fear is something nature gives us for our own protection, and yet one of the earliest sentiments we hear from our parents is, "Don't be afraid." Fortunately, most of us learn to strike a balance between excessive fear and none at all, but some families are so extreme on the subject that they direct their children into a lifetime of denial. Many children—especially sons—are humiliated for being frightened. If they run home crying after being beaten up by the school bully, they're sent back to "fight it out." Sometimes they're commanded to be "brave" and to dive into the swimming pool or ride the bike without the training wheels. Then, when they hang back in fear, they're taunted for being weak or cowardly or downright sissyish, and some of them spend their whole lives attempting to prove they're none of those things. They become the chance-takers among us, driving like maniacs, skiing in bad conditions, hang-gliding, skydiving, and placing all their emphasis on "being a real man."

Morton's Story

These are not ordinary sports enthusiasts I'm talking about. These are extremists who set out to tempt fate and then brag about their superhuman exploits so the world will know how brave they are. Often they convince the world, but they never seem to convince themselves, and they persist in taking increasingly risky chances, sometimes on a physical plane, sometimes not. Many men wheel and deal themselves into danger on a

financial level. I had a case just recently. A young man
we'll call Morton came to see me because his life had
been threatened and he wanted some pointers on "the
best psychological way to handle the situation." He
wanted to know what I could suggest. He looked and
sounded quite nonchalant, and when I suggested he go
to the police, he was quick to assure me that he could
take care of his own problems and that only a weakling
would call in the authorities. The only reason he had
come to me was that he wanted to give himself an edge
by taking the right psychological approach.

I won't turn this into a cliff-hanger by making you
wait to find out if Morton got himself killed. He didn't.
But the story of how he got into such a predicament is
interesting and helps to demonstrate what the denial of
fear can do to us. Morton's father was a successful
businessman, a powerful force in his industry, and very
wealthy. He had always primed Morton to be "tough"
and "to stand on his own two feet," although as a child,
Morton hadn't quite known what those terms meant.
Not until he left college and went to work for his father
did he realize that his father had always thought of him
as not being "manly" enough. No matter what Morton
did, it didn't measure up to his father's standards, according to which Morton was too soft in negotiations,
didn't drive a hard enough bargain, backed down too
easily, and would never amount to anything.

Finally, Morton had had it. He took some money
that had come to him when he was twenty-one and set
out to show his father how "tough" he could be. Morton was bright and had he been more temperate, he
might have been successful, but because he was
wrongly motivated, he got himself into a mess. Determined to outwheel and outdeal his father, he plunged
into the first venture that came along. It happened to be
a disco, about which Morton knew nothing except that
it was more glamorous than his father's business. Besides, with the disco craze going at full blast, he was
sure he'd have a flashy success. He had some reservations about the men who would be his partners, but
didn't stop to investigate them with anything even akin

to thoroughness. He put up half his share of the investment with a promise to pay the other half out of his profits, but there *were* no profits, and his partners turned out to be very narrow-minded about debts. You either paid or else.

Morton was in real danger when he came to see me, and yet he continued to act with bravado, which is why deniers of fear are such a menace to themselves and why they burn themselves out—if they don't kill themselves first. The denial act impairs their judgment, and they tend to make rash decisions. Despite all the evidence to the contrary, Morton insisted he'd be able to talk his way out of trouble. "I'm not scared of them," he kept saying. I pointed out a number of times that he *ought* to be scared, that he was dealing with hoodlums, and that he would be wise to go to his father and borrow money. Morton flatly refused, because although he would never have admitted it, he was more afraid of his father than of anyone or anything else in this world.

With the deadline for payment fast approaching, there was no time to get Morton to weigh the relative gravity of the two threats and do the sensible thing. Instead, I prevailed upon him to go to his mother's brother, a suggestion he took only because his father and uncle weren't on speaking terms. Even when the incident was settled, Morton continued to point out that he had never been afraid, but that I had made such a fuss he felt he might as well do something. It was many, many months before he saw that he had come to me in the first place out of fear. When his therapy finally helped him to break through his denial, he said to me, as if it were a completely new idea. "Y'know, I must have been crazy. I could have been killed."

Denial of Age. Wherever you go these days, you almost cannot turn around without bumping into someone who's denying getting older. The fifty-year-old swinger with a twenty-year-old on his arm has become a cliché. So have the face-lift and the breast-lift and the tummy-tuck. It's as if everyone is trying to be twenty-six again. Well, let's face it, nobody loves the prospect of getting old (except those who, as the saying goes, consider the alternative!), but some of us are so pathologically afraid of it, we burn ourselves out in a vain attempt to ward off both the real and the anticipated effects of aging.

As a man gets into his late forties and fifties, he sees younger, more ambitious people moving up on the corporate ladder, and he panics. "Maybe," he thinks, "they'll be able to do more than I can. Maybe they'll have newer, fresher viewpoints. Maybe they're here to replace me." He begins to work harder than he worked when he was younger, often putting a Burn-Out into motion by stretching himself beyond his capacity.

Not that his fears are unjustified. On the contrary, they're direct reflections of the values of our society. Corporations *do* replace older executives; husbands *do* leave their wives for younger women. Since the sixties, we've been living in a youth-oriented culture which sends forth the message that younger is better. Nevertheless, since we obviously can't escape the aging process, it's futile to deny it's taking place. The aging executive who sets up an active competition with younger staff members does himself a great disservice. In trying to match a younger energy level, he raises youth to a rank of prime importance, at the same time devaluating qualities like judgment and experience, in which he probably excels. Whereas other people might not have been making comparisons at all, he almost forces them to, just as an overly made-up, youthfully dressed matron invites unflattering comparisons in a roomful of young beauties. When we deny, we damage ourselves. Not only do we exhaust our systems by placing extra burdens on them, we also point up our deficiencies and downplay our strengths. It is almost axiomatic that the individual strongly ruled by denial brings about what he is trying hardest to forestall.

A doctor friend of mine who had been hugely successful all his life and was now the senior member of a flourishing medical group fell into the denial trap when he reached his sixtieth birthday. All of a sudden, as if someone had pushed a button, this dynamic, robust man began acting like a novice fighting a battle for position. Whereas the group had been formed around him for the express purpose of using his outstanding diagnostic skills, he was now unavailable when they needed him because he was out taking every call, no matter how routine. When his colleagues tried to point out to him that he was usurping other people's territory, working unnecessarily long hours, and generally disrupting the entire organization, he grew furious, accusing the others of goofing off and forcing him into this position. My friend's story is sad. He persisted in misusing his resources so thoroughly that even his diagnostic powers suffered and his colleagues felt they had no recourse but to ask him to leave the group. He is now a bitter old man of sixty-one instead of the functioning, energetic man he would have remained had he not denied himself into a Burn-Out. One more victim of our society's youth fetish!

People who age well are the ones who acknowledge aging, not the ones who deny it. They accommodate themselves to each successive decade instead of clinging to past ones. Does this mean they let themselves go, stop caring about their appearance, put themselves out to pasture, so to speak? Not at all. Rather, it means that because they can see aging in a positive as well as a negative light they behave appropriately and with common sense. They develop new skills and continue to work to capacity, but don't feel constantly compelled to compete in the province of vigor. They also keep themselves looking good and staying fit, but always in ways that enhance who and what they are. They feel no compulsion to rival an Olympics training program or a Follies chorus line.

Many older people, in contrast to my doctor friend, embrace innovations and new methods, rather than putting them down. They admire young people, find them lively, and like to be in their company. I know people past eighty who still do part-time work just to keep active and in touch. They're aware that the world has changed since it was "their" world, but that doesn't upset them. Rather, it keeps them curious, eager to see

what's going to happen next. Such people are not deniers; they are affirmers of who and what they are, willing to make the most of each stage of life instead of
trying to cling vainly to their youth.

People who are denying getting older have a tendency to live in the past. "We were better then. More
reliable. More responsible. Harder working." "We took
pride in our work, didn't goof off, didn't look for shortcuts all the time." Movies were better. Books were better. We all know people who refute progress, as if to
admit it would be to repudiate themselves. And what do
they accomplish? They take themselves farther and farther from the mainstream of life, becoming both spiritu-
ally and physically older than their years. To rephrase
what I said before: Denial intensifies that which is
being denied.

Denial of Death. Perhaps the most intense form of denial concerns itself with death, the inevitable end
against which we play out the whole of our lives. Death
is a frightening concept, there's no disputing that. From
the time we're first confronted with it as small children,
we cannot help but wonder, "What is it like?" "Will it
hurt?" "Will we be lonely and scared?" As we grow
older, we become frightened in another sense. All those
things we wanted to do. Will there be time? Or will we
be snatched away before we accomplish a particular
goal or before we find happiness? Besides, if we're
going to die anyway, what difference does it make what
we do or how we act? Death is a very sobering thought
to humankind and has been to every society we have
traces of.

Death and its attendant fears have been sources of
every mythology and religion. Rituals, gods, visions of
an afterlife, reincarnation are constantly invented and
reinvented to mitigate man's terror. We also do our best
to minimize our concerns about death by establishing
goals, making plans, concerning ourselves with future
generations, and surrounding ourselves with people who
love us and have the power to make us feel immortal.
When we involve ourselves actively in life and living,

thoughts of death don't preoccupy or frighten us. They're somewhere within our consciousness, but we're too busy participating and caring to worry much about being cut off "in our prime." That's a mild form of denial, and a positive one which serves most of us well.

Some people, however, are haunted by the specter of death. They are ruled by it as surely as the rest of us are ruled by the life force. That is not to say they have a "death wish" or an eagerness to die; it's to explain that while life pulls the majority of human beings into its center with its own equivalent of a centripetal force, it doesn't seem to swoop up these others. Perhaps this is so because those individuals have never entered into life wholeheartedly, some event or force having kept them detached and disengaged.

People who hold themselves aloof from life worry that death will overtake them before they've really lived. Sometimes they act on this worry by impeding their ability to live even further. They stay away from parties because they might catch a cold; they won't fly on airplanes because there might be a crash. Others, however, go to the opposite extreme. They dare death, defy it, tempt it in every way they can think of, as if to say, "I'm not afraid of you. You can't scare me." This is an extreme, unhealthy form of denial, and it appears often in people from homes where illness and dying were significant factors when they were young. Someone who saw a sibling die early or whose parent became an invalid may become obsessed with proving that nothing like that will ever happen to him. He turns himself into a superdoer, never tired, never ill, taking more risks even than their denier of fear.

Not too long ago, a patient of mine who prides himself on being "in perfect health," "even stronger now" at fifty-eight than he had been in his twenties, came down with pneumonia. His medical doctor cautioned him that it was serious and he must stay home from work for several weeks. "You're pretty run down," the doctor told him. "Been working too hard. We're not as young as we used to be, you know. It's time to start pampering yourself a little." The doctor might as well

have waved a red flag in front of a bull. Within a week,
the man was back at work and into his usual pursuits,
including several sessions of duplicate bridge a week.
At one of them, he collapsed and had to be taken, by
ambulance, to the hospital.

Many people go so overboard in their denial of death
that this becomes their vehicle for burning themselves
out. I've seen it happen to young men and women as
well as to those who are past middle age. A twenty-
seven-year-old account executive who had been fired
from a well-paying job at an advertising agency had a
strong memory of how his father had once been fired
and then had gone into a sharp decline from which he
had not recovered. The memory, although vivid, was
not accurate (he had compressed two episodes into
one), but the young man had carried it with him for
many years, and in his head being fired equated with
dying.

This, of course, was an equation he had to prove
wrong, and his way of doing that was to plunge into
daredevil activities. He took up a form of skateboarding
so dangerous it required a helmet. In special, man-
made configurations that curved and plummeted like
one of the wildest rides at an amusement park, he spent
his afternoons whirling up and down arcs of more than
180 degrees. Fortunately, he broke a leg before he had
a chance to kill himself, and this sobered him sufficiently to help me get him to look at what he was doing.

When older people behave in reckless ways, it's often
because they've seen several of their contemporaries
succumb to fatal illnesses, and they want to remove
themselves as far as possible from identification with
that age group. "Well, he was an *old* sixty-two," they
tell themselves. "I'm still jogging [or swimming, or hik-
ing] three miles a day." A sixty-five-year-old woman,
the mother of one of my patients, was always doing
something rash. At a time when she was not yet fully
recovered from a broken collarbone that she had in-
curred ice-skating, she went canoeing down the rapids
in Colorado. My patient had begged her not to go, reminding her that her collarbone was not yet healed, and

she might not be as strong as she thought she was. "Oh you just think I'm too old," the mother rejoined. "Well, I'm not. I've got as much spunk as I ever had. And besides, what has my collarbone got to do with canoeing?" As it turned out . . . a lot. The woman didn't have enough power in her arms to hold onto the ropes, and she ended her trip with a brain concussion.

All around us, people are running from death with a vengeance, but in such crazy ways that they can more truly be said to be courting it. There's a marvelous folk story that has been told and retold for hundreds of years. It was used by Somerset Maugham in a play and it served John O'Hara as the title of his novel *Appointment in Samarra*. The legend tells of a merchant in Baghdad who sent his servant to market. The servant returned, frightened, and told his master he had seen Death in the marketplace and Death had looked at him in a threatening way. He begged his master to lend him a horse so he could ride to Samarra and "avoid his fate." After he was gone, the master went to the marketplace. He saw Death there and asked why Death had threatened his servant. "I did not threaten him," Death answered. "I was merely expressing my surprise. I was astonished to see him in Baghdad, for I had an appointment with him tonight in Samarra."

False Cures

≈

People embark on denial as a way of avoiding the pain that comes from facing their fears. It takes a lot of courage to look at unpleasantness squarely, as you probably know from your own experience. First, you have to acknowledge that something crucial to your well-being is going wrong. Then you have to assess how much of it is your fault. That's probably the hardest part of all, but calming yourself and finding a sensible way to straighten matters out can be almost as difficult. You may have to ask for advice and, when you get it, follow it. You have to do a fair amount of reality testing to evaluate your alternatives and to measure what the worst possible consequence will be if the dreaded event comes to pass.

Certainly it's easier, especially at first, to deny there's a problem at all, and sometimes that works. Denial is not categorically bad. Many minor upsets, left to their own devices, fade away, whereas if we had plunged in immediately to do something about them, we might have made them worse. Only when we employ denial misguidedly or to excess does it corrode us. Appropriately applied, it is a useful mechanism for helping us get through life.

As we all discover at an early age, being human isn't easy; much of life is frightening and sad. Our "best-laid schemes . . . gang aft a-gley," particularly those of potential Burn-Outs, whose plans are apt to be long-range and elaborate. Despite their uncommon ability and the high goals they set for themselves, unexpected disappointments and detours crop up: Spouses die or ask for divorces; children rebel against the life-styles their parents have worked so hard to provide; bosses don't necessarily appreciate the extra effort of a job well done; bureaucracy blocks the rapid advancement the achiever feels he has earned. On a philosophical level, we know that we were born to die and that our individual lives don't mean much in the over-all scheme of the universe. We look at a mountain or the vast night sky and are reminded of our relative insignificance. Yet as flesh-and-blood creatures, we want to invest our lives with meaning, and it's healthy and positive that we should. But how do we go about it when we're so tiny and the cosmos is so tremendous? We call upon denial and other coping devices to help us cut the world down to a manageable size.

No individual can cope with everything the world serves up. It's too vast. For our own survival, we have to turn portions of it off, particularly death. If we were constantly bogged down by considerations of our mortality, real as they are, we could never get on with the business of living, so we tuck those considerations away and devote our energies to matters we know we can handle. Again, that's healthy and positive, an instance of denial used in a life-enhancing way. Instead of paralyzing ourselves by worrying over something we can't do anything about, we make use of the time we *do* have to lead as rich and full a life as we're capable of. As I mentioned before, we insulate ourselves from the specter of death by working, playing, loving, living, and procreating. We de-emphasize death by not leaving time for it in our thoughts or by ritualizing it into something less frightening, a process that has always been a function of religion from the most primitive mythologies to the most highly developed systems.

In times of deep faith, mankind is able to achieve the ultimate in denial by embracing the belief that this life is merely a prelude to eternity, that death is not an ending at all but the most desirable of beginnings. "We may be mortal in this sphere," we convince ourselves, "but we'll be immortal when we get to Heaven." By placing ourselves in God's hands and substituting faith for fear, we virtually banish death and make our lives easier to bear. A big reason our lives are more difficult today and more prone to Burn-Out is our repudiation of religion and the buffers it provides for dealing with uncomfortable issues and situations.

Because we no longer accept explanations of faith and have not yet formulated satisfactory communal substitutes, we have to improvise our own solutions to every problem that comes along, even the trivial disappointments of daily living. This is not only difficult, it's also confusing and burdensome. Since we have no precedents, each of us develops a life plan consistent with our capacity to deal with difficulties: If we're strong, we extend our horizons in many directions; if we find multiple concerns overwhelming, we eliminate all but the most basic. Either way, the principle is the same: We tailor our lives to fit us, intuitively structuring and circumscribing our boundaries to cushion "the thousand natural shocks that flesh is heir to." We use denial to lighten our load so it won't end up crushing us. Our defenses can be as simple as turning on the television set to blot out a bad day at the office or as subtle as developing an illness to avoid facing that we have no friends. But always, what we're attempting to do is block out larger anxieties by concentrating on concerns that don't frighten us as much. In this way, denial is a manifestation of our instinct for self-preservation.

DULLING AND DEADNESS

Once denial becomes obsessive, however, and crosses over the line into dulling and deadness, it can only work against us. If we're having all we can do to feed our families, it makes sense for us to close our minds to the problem of starvation in India. That's setting ourselves a realistic limitation. Since we can't afford to dissipate our energies worrying about global issues when we have a crisis at home, we're restricting our concerns appropriately. By blotting out what we can't change anyway, we're giving ourselves a chance to solve the immediate problem. As our concerns become smaller, we feel more able to tackle them, and in that way, denial fortifies us.

It is quite another matter, however, to resist something so thoroughly that we always have to be on guard against it, protecting ourselves with substitutes or distancing devices like taking to our beds because we're pathologically afraid of catching the flu that's going around, or drinking ourselves into a stupor to avoid admitting that our marriage is a failure. That kind of denial is akin to paralysis. We're not mustering our strength for action; we're simply taking flight in a passive manner, hoping that if we ignore whatever is bothering us, it will go away. Unfortunately, it usually won't. At best, denial can ameliorate our pain for a little while, but it soon ceases to be effective, and we require heavier, and still heavier, doses of cover-up. That's when we venture into the more dangerous precincts of the False Cures, using any means we have at hand: alcohol, drugs, gambling, sex, excessive work or sports or games.

As we saw in Martha's story, a terrible thing happens when we attempt to dull and deaden our pain: We dull and deaden ourselves. It's like taking a pain killer to cure a toothache. We may anesthetize our systems for a while and feel better temporarily, but the decay is still flourishing underneath and will flare up again in due time. If we continue to dope ourselves, we'll create havoc in two ways: We'll allow the decaying tooth to get worse, and we'll become dependent upon the drug. Camouflage is not a cure. No matter what form it takes, it can't get rid of a problem; it can only mask it. And while it's never strong enough to do the job we want it to do, it always has powerful side effects that rob us of our vitality.

When she first became unhappy, Martha immersed herself in what she had been told was her "duty." She hoped that if she turned into a first-rate mother and homemaker, she'd start to feel good again. But how could those roles possibly have restored her self-esteem when she placed no value on them? What they did, instead, was force Martha to stifle her feelings so thoroughly that she became robotlike. Far from feeling better, she felt progressively worse and worse, until she was willing to abandon her husband and child in the hope of recapturing her sense of aliveness. Her involvement with her young man was simply another opiate, and had she gone off with him, she'd soon have found *that* remedy insufficient as well.

If you have reached a state of dulling and deadness similar to Martha's, it's wise—and imperative to your well-being—to try tracing it to its source. You're undoubtedly burning out for some reason, and if you let this kind of lassitude or withdrawal go unchecked, it will intensify. The more recent these feelings (or nonfeelings) are, the more easily the problem will come to light, but even if they're of long standing, you can get to the core of them with a little perseverance.

Once again, pick a quiet place, preferably when you're alone in the house. Get your pad or, if you have one, a tape recorder. Tape is ideal for this particular probe, because listening to your voice will be very revealing. You may be astonished to hear how you sound. Take some time over each question, giving thought to specific instances where you *did* notice something, but then dismissed it. Remember, you're looking for two things: (1) Is something wrong? (2) Am I trying to put it out of my mind?

1. Are you plugging away at something you don't enjoy doing? (your job, a relationship, your role in the family)

2. Have you discussed your feelings with anyone or are even the people closest to you unaware of your conflict?

3. Do you have to force yourself to do routine things? (taking care of your clothes, being polite, finishing chores you've started)

4. Do you feel listless and always in search of diversion?

5. Would you constantly like to be somewhere else, whether you're at a party or at work?

6. Has sex become more of a burden than a pleasure?

7. Are you having more to drink now than you used to? (even if it's only one!)

8. Do you need a tranquilizer to keep you from screaming during the day? Or a sleeping pill to help you get some rest at night?

9. Do you feel resigned, rather than enthusiastic, about your future?

10. Is your need for a particular crutch increasing? (such as smoking, eating, nail biting, pot)

Once you've answered the questions, try to estimate how different you are now from the way you used to be. Then see if you can figure out when the differences began. Pinpointing a time may lead you directly to the source of the trouble, no matter how securely you've locked it away. Pay particular attention to those *first* extra drinks or packages of cigarettes or prescriptions for tranquilizers or extra hours at work. They're probably your strongest clues to when you became sufficiently distressed about something to try to push it out of your mind. Be prepared to make an effort, particularly if you reacted positively to several of the questions, because denial, by its very nature, strips us of our ability to admit things easily. Those people who end up in advanced cases of Burn-Out are the ones who never forced themselves to check their behavior and feelings and what they signified.

WHERE DENIAL LEADS

Paul's Story

Paul was one of those people. He had let denial rule his life and had become so accustomed to being at a distance from his feelings that he thought the rest of the world lived that way. Paul always saw only what he wanted to, which is the equivalent of living a lie. And so, when the truth flared up and forced itself upon him, he was totally unprepared for it. Because he had been denying himself insights throughout the years and allowing himself to take everything at face value, the explosion that finally came blew him apart.

The first time Paul walked into my office, he was so drunk he could hardly sit through his appointed hour. If you had seen his disheveled appearance and heard his slurred speech, you'd have thought he had wandered in from Skid Row. Only the fact that he had been referred to me by the director of personnel of a large corporation kept me from pegging him as a habitual nonachiever who had been flouting convention and the work ethic all his life. Weeks of probing and listening to his story confirmed the opposite, however. Paul was not a derelict, but a Burn-Out who had turned to alcoholism as an escape from his despair and was now burning himself out even further through his chosen remedy.

Paul's entire history was one of doing the "right thing." He had been born into a respectable, churchgoing family who set high goals for their children, and he had never let them down. He got good grades in Catholic elementary schools, graduated from Notre Dame, landed a job with a good company, married, and fathered two children. Without ever reviewing the pertinency of his parents' goals, he perpetuated them in his own marriage and career. Life in Paul's home was not much different from life in his father's house.

Paul never had the spectacular career he had hoped for, but he worked his way up the corporate ladder by being conscientious and fitting into the organization. He knew how to play the game, and he played it. He dressed properly, arrived early, and stayed late. Even when he was frustrated and chafing at the bit to rebel against time-wasting procedures, he restrained his impulses, reminding himself that his primary goal was maintaining his family's way of life. Responsibility became Paul's driving force, and by placing everything else secondary to it, he eventually attained a vice presidency and a fifty-five-thousand-dollar salary.

That title should have been a high spot in Paul's life, but the day it came through, he forgot to tell his wife about it, let alone take her out to celebrate. Although he had always expected it to be the culmination of his career, the announcement and the few minutes in the president's office had seemed dreary. Like Miriam after opening night, he felt let down. Much like her, he said, "I don't know exactly what I expected, but after all this time, there should have been more to it." I asked Paul if he had been having fun "all this time," but he had never stopped to ask himself. Nor had his wife, Anna. Both of them were so fixated on the trappings of "good living" they never looked beneath the surface to check for things like happiness or fun. Anna took the children to church, encouraged them to behave and do well in school, and cooked nourishing meals. She accompanied her husband to business functions when her presence was required, and she managed the house with no problems or complaints when he was off on a business trip.

As a family, Paul and Anna were fulfilling all the time-honored American goals, focusing on the pretty picture they and their children made and denying any cracks in the paint. Paul had his few drinks every evening and Anna took her occasional sleeping pill, but all in all, they had no complaints about life. When they found evidence that their sixteen-year-old son was on pot, they reacted in their customary way. Since it didn't fit in with their picture, they simply refused to believe it. "Not possible," they thought, "not in our family."

Drugs happened to other people . . . in slums, on TV, maybe to that unconventional family down the block. But certainly not to them. They put the entire episode out of their minds until young Paul was picked up for dealing in heroin, and then they had no choice. They were forced to acknowledge the situation.

Their whole world collapsed. Anna resorted to tranquilizers and barbiturates; Paul to drink. Arguments and accusations flew between them. Their son's trouble had stripped away their flimsy façade and exposed how meaningless those surface trappings, with no substantial foundation under them, had always been. By dragging his parents into the police station, young Paul had repudiated all their strivings, and they had nothing else to draw upon for support.

What had gone wrong? What had caused this apparently happy family to explode into little pieces? Why didn't they have sufficient resources to meet the crisis without falling apart? In working with Paul, I came to see clearly that he had spent his adult years striving to perpetuate a way of life he had neither devised nor questioned. The real Paul and his authentic desires had been submerged to the point of nonexistence, and he had formed his family's life-style out of pictures. A pleasant home. A cohesive group. Good manners. Clean living. And because he had bought these pictures on good authority (his church, his parents, his community), he accepted them the same way a novice art collector accepts the authentication of an expert. During his entire married life, Paul had never taken a real look at what was happening in his household. If he had, he'd have noticed that his son had been sending out signals for help for a long time. As it was, however, the people in his house were completely out of touch. They were as much strangers to each other as if they had lived separately.

OTHER-DIRECTEDNESS

This kind of barren living is a direct result of "other-directedness," a condition that arises wherever denial flourishes. At the two extremes of finding a path to follow through life stand our own natural desires and the desires—or constraints—of the world around us. Often the two are in conflict, and in the process of growing, we make concessions to both in varying degrees until we hit upon a satisfactory middle ground. Those who are incapable of compromise stay locked in one of the extremes. Either they become totally self-indulgent and antisocial, riding roughshod over others in a psychopathic fashion, or they become "other-directed," stamping out their own motivating forces and supplanting them almost entirely by dicta from outside themselves.

All of us who aren't criminals or the psychic equivalent make concessions to society. Many of our actions are governed by the world around us rather than by our own preferences. We wear clothes, we don't defecate in the street, we refrain from shooting people because the law takes a dim view of such behavior. We also very often put other people's pleasure ahead of our own, but usually such behavior represents a conscious choice. When we become other-directed, however, we've ceased to know what we want to do; we need to have others tell us. We've become victims of that separation from one's self which we talked about earlier. We have, first of all, lost touch with our feelings, and second, lost a sense of our own self-worth.

Other-directedness is such a commonplace that in large organizations you can always tell the pecking order at a meeting by watching everyone's eyes. Each person there will be looking to the person just higher for agreement. You can almost see the wheels moving. "Do you want me to say 'yes' to that or would it be better if I said 'no'? Maybe 'We'll get back to you tomorrow' would be even better." This happens in family

life, too: children, even spouses, glancing nervously to
their "authority figure" before they'll answer a question
or make a decision.

In Paul's case, other-directedness had set in early,
and Paul had submerged his life preferences so thoroughly that by the time I met him, they were all but
forgotten. Had it not been for a chance observation on
my part, we might never have brought them to the surface at all. What happened was this: Several times,
when I went into the waiting room to greet Paul and
bring him into my office, I noticed that he was humming. I would hear him as I approached the room, and
again as we walked toward the office. I began to listen
for it, and sure enough, whenever I had to take a telephone call and Paul was left to himself for a minute or
two, the humming would start. One day, when I put
down the phone, I said to Paul, "Pretty tune. What is
it?" He looked around as if I had been addressing
someone else. He had no idea what I was talking about.
I told him he had been humming, and he laughed. "Not
me," he said with certainty. "I never hum. I don't even
listen to music."

Paul's protests notwithstanding, the humming continued. I knew it was an important clue to something Paul
had blocked out a long time ago, something which, like
the humming, he was completely oblivious to. Whatever
it was, I had to make him aware of it, so I introduced a
few minutes of silence into our sessions, explaining to
Paul that, like meditation, silence is often enlightening.
Just as I thought he would, he hummed the whole time.
Next time we met, I had a tape recorder, which Paul
knew nothing about, all set to record, and when our
quiet time was over, I played the recording for Paul.
The effect was profound. He was in turn startled, unbe-
lieving, nostalgic, and sad. He identified the music as a
Mozart violin concerto he had practiced for months
some thirty years ago and never thought of since.

After weeks of fruitless talking, we were finally on to
something. Paul had been introduced to music in a
school program and had taken to it immediately. He
loved practicing the violin, especially when the music

teacher singled him out for his talent and encouraged him to audition for a special high school. The problem was Paul's father, who didn't want any son of his involved in such a frivolous pursuit. He was dead set against Paul's having anything to do with music, called him a sissy, and let it be known in no uncertain terms that only fags played the violin. Paul was crushed. He never went for the audition, not did he ever play again. His way of handling the episode was to banish it, along with music, from his consciousness. The Paul I met owned no records and hadn't been to a concert since he was a boy.

Interestingly enough, Paul's denial was so effective that he unwittingly passed his father's message on to young Paul. Not in the same way, since there was no instrument involved, but in the sense, "In our family, we don't waste our time on frivolous things like music." When young Paul and his friends got "hooked" on rock, collecting records and listening to them for hours on end, Paul became livid. He confiscated the records and forbade his son to bring "that noise" into the house. "Study. Be something," he lectured. "That's how a man behaves. I don't sit around wasting my time all day, and I don't expect you to." These were his father's sentiments exactly, and yet Paul had never made the connection. Now, for the first time, he was able to see how gravely he had deprived himself of something he loved and how he had extended the deprivation to his son. If he had not gained these insights, he would never have understood how he had contributed to his son's drug problem.

So, then, other-directedness means denying who and what we are and molding ourselves anew according to some externally imposed standard. Because we no longer trust ourselves to validate our own choices and accomplishments, we turn to outside sources for approval and standards, becoming dependent on others to the point where we can't even take pleasure in a job well done unless someone else puts his sanction on it. The more we look to others for validation, the more likely we are to subject ourselves to Burn-Out, because we're not pleasing ourselves in any true sense. All we're allowing ourselves to feel is a reflection of somebody else's pleasure. We can't function wholly if we disenfranchise ourselves from our own beings and measure our happiness through other people's eyes.

That's what Anna and Paul had been doing—judging themselves according to what the world might be thinking of them. They were preoccupied with questions of show. Was the house big enough? Did they know the right people? Were their children popular and headed for prestige colleges? With all this frantic concentration on appearances, their inner beings had become so shut away they scarcely noticed what was happening to their minds, bodies, feelings, integrity, closeness, and authentic relatedness. While Paul and Anna had always seemed to be busy, devoted parents, their industry had always been misdirected. Paul was away from home a lot, traveling for his company, attending meetings, volunteering to run training sessions and entertain clients. Anna, on the other hand, was always at home. But what had she been doing? Papering and painting the house, cleaning, gardening—not sharing activities with her children.

Had Anna and Paul been building up real values all these years, they would have had the fortication they needed to face the major problem that arose and find answers. They could have helped their son look into the feelings and fears that had led him to drugs and emerged a stronger, healthier unit. As it was, however, they had developed no positive coping devices. Denial, which Paul had always relied on, wasn't strong enough for a problem of this magnitude. It had to be reinforced in some way, and so Paul increased his drinking. Being "out of it" was easier for him than thinking of what the neighbors must be saying and what the arrest would do to young Paul's chances of getting into college.

Not surprisingly, since it's always the case with a "false cure," the drinking didn't help, but simply got heavier until Paul was unable to contain it. It went from evenings to lunches to a bottle in the desk drawer until the director of personnel stepped in and sent Paul to me. Finally, he had no alternative but to face everything he had spent his adult life denying: that some critical dimension was missing in the world he had structured for himself and his family. All the striving, the respectable career, the "proper" way of life, the aspirations for the children had been no more than coverups for the dulling and deadness that had existed all along and flared up during the crisis.

Had Paul's choices been authentic, they would have animated the household, sparking family contact and discussions and a general sense of purpose. Because they were other-directed and therefore *in*authentic, they generated, instead, an apathy which led first to the son's use of drugs, then to Paul's drinking.

That's an important sequence, so let's follow it for a moment. Although it may seem, on the surface, that the father's drinking problem was caused by his son's arrest, to understand Paul's story we must recognize that *both* problems were the outgrowth of apathy. If we examine the dynamics of the family situation, we can see that Paul's habitual despondency had infected his son, and young Paul was in effect acting out what he sensed and reacted to so keenly in his father. Young Paul's explosion happened to come first, but the order could easily have been reversed, since pressure had been building up inside both of them simultaneously. Paul had been on a Burn-Out course for years, taking his whole family with him. His son's arrest triggered Paul's drinking in much the same way that Archduke Ferdinand's assassination triggered World War I: They were both immediate and precipitating events, but only because more profound grievances had been festering unchecked for a long time. The arrest served to speed up Paul's alcoholic timetable; nothing more.

THE FALSE CURES

As people experience anesthesia of feeling, they flail out at anything that seems capable of eliciting a response within them. Living in a numbed state is so intolerable that even pursuits an individual once considered immoral become desirable as long as they promise feeling. In the beginning, however, most people turn, as Martha did, to an intensification of what has been causing their distress in the first place. If work is disappointing them, they try more work, looking for greater and greater achievement. Somewhere along the line, they reason, it's bound to start feeling good. They become relentless in their pursuit of accomplishment, power, status, education, or money in the hope that one of these will bring exhilaration. Haven't they been told all their lives that achievement is the panacea? Like Miriam they think, "Just one level higher, and it will appear."

Should work fail to produce the desired result, what then? A shot of alcohol, a dose of drugs, a plunge into forbidden sexuality, a foray into gambling. As if to convince themselves they're still alive, young and old alike are diving into activities that must, by their very nature, become more and more excessive to fill the void. On every front, people are relying on constant charges to revitalize them, continuous excitement as a substitute for genuine fulfillment.

Now, in case you're wondering, "What's wrong with excitement?" let me be quick to assure you: not a thing. Nor is there anything wrong with *any* pursuit in and of itself. Pleasure in all its forms is an animating force and most of us take our pleasures where we find them. If our work is a source of satisfaction over and above its primary function of providing us with a livelihood, it enriches us twice as much. If we go out jogging to stay in shape and find that it's an exhilarating way to take our minds off our troubles and work out some of our tensions, we get a lot more out of jogging. Enjoyment is an essential part of a well-rounded life, no matter what form it takes. Television, that much-maligned "idiot box," can be put to beneficial use when we need some convenient distraction. Sex, of course, serves us on a thousand levels. You have only to look at our magazines, books, and movies to see how large a part sex plays in our society. Undoubtedly, gambling, alcohol, the occasional sleeping pill, even pornography all have their places in our lives as long as we call upon them in moderation.

People who exlude pleasure and distraction from their lives become bored and boring, steeped in the earnestness of existence. We all need relief now and then from the realities of our daily routines. When diversions are supplements to our more serious activities, they supply us with exactly what we're looking for—a bit of fun, a change of pace, an excitement that renews our energies. Because they contribute to our aliveness, they have a therapeutic value, and as long as they remain proportionate to the other areas of our lives, there is no danger in them. It's only when that hidden villain, Burn-Out, is at work deep within that the trouble starts.

This may be a good time for you to look at some of your distractions to see whether you're controlling them or they're controlling you.

Take a sheet of paper—a legal-size pad would be perfect—and jot down the things you do for diversion. List them all, whether they sound like False Cures to you or not. They can be healthy pursuits, like jogging or swimming or tennis or golf. They can be "just things you do," like smoking, nail biting, or daydreaming. Eating. Reading. Television watching. Movies. Records. Disco evenings. Consider them all. Gambling is important, whether it's the office football pool or the lottery or trips to the track. Liquor. Pills. Pot. Whatever you do for distraction, excitement, or escape.

Once you've made your list, and it can consist of one or many, keep it handy. Get into the habit of paying attention to whatever is on it. For instance, when you start to think about an item on the list, make a note. Keep track of how long it has been occupying your mind. A minute, a quarter of an hour? Note how many times a day it pops up. About the same as always? Or increasingly?

Notice, too, if you're peppering your conversation with references to it (or them). If you are, keep count of the frequency.

Go over your routines and check for changes. Are you seeing different people these days? Discarding old friends for new ones who share your enthusiasm? (A doctor I know became a quaalude abuser, using samples at first and an occasional prescription. As he became more dependent on the drug, he was afraid he'd be spotted, so he turned to illegal channels. His supplier was a disreputable character from out of town, and he took to dropping in to see the doctor even when he wasn't making a delivery. Soon the doctor's wife was asking questions. "Who is that person?" "A colleague from upstate." "That man is a doctor? What hospital is he affiliated with?" The wife soon uncovered the story, and lucky for her husband she did, because if much more time had gone by, he'd have been totally burned out or worse.)

Pay careful attention to whether you're letting things other than your preoccupation go. Think about haircuts, laundry, getting your clothes to the cleaner, shopping for food, paying bills, billing clients, returning phone calls, answering your mail, even reading your mail, keeping in touch with friends.

If you seem to be slipping in some of these categories, remember whether you've been forgetting important occasions. (One of my patients, an addicted gambler, had a horse in the third race the day of his best friend's father's funeral. My patient had practically been raised by this man, his own father having died when he was very young, yet the funeral completely slipped his mind, and he spent the day at the track. His friend has not spoken to him since.)

All this examining may seem like a lot of fuss to make over "a little something" in your life. But it's far easier to cut something off when it's still little. If you don't take stock now, your distraction may get out of hand and propel you into a full-fledged Burn-Out.

False Cures II

❧

This is a good place to stop for a moment to remind ourselves of our composite portrait of a Burn-Out candidate. We said that he is charismatic, energetic, impatient, and given to high standards, throwing himself into whatever he does with all his might, expecting it to provide rewards commensurate with the effort spent. We've also said that the times we live in conspire against those among us who have high expectations. As our work settings become larger and larger, we feel smaller and smaller. Our jobs are often fractionalized to the point where we never see the results of our efforts or even feel like a member of the team. Our governments, both local and federal, have become so mammoth we often have no idea who our representatives are, let alone whether or not they're representing us. The money we worked so hard for and set aside so assiduously is worth less every day, and no matter how provident we have tried to be, we now have to worry all over again about a nest egg for our retirement.

The striver feels beset on all sides. His frustrations mount until they're too painful to contain, and he has to try to make himself comfortable. Perhaps, as Paul had been doing all along, he takes a drink or two, and the world looks a little better. Nothing wrong with that . . . at least in most instances. We just said, a few paragraphs ago, that "everybody" does that kind of thing. It *can* be dangerous for the person who is burning out, however, because he brings the same personality traits, the same behavior patterns to his remedy that he

brought to his previous interest and which led him to
Burn-Out in the first place. The problem is that a
Burn-Out isn't a moderate. Whatever he does, he does
it to the hilt, and he will immerse himself in his new
regimen as totally as he did in his original one.

The Burn-Out personality thrives on intensity. Often
his life is set up so that he lurches from crisis to crisis,
because he functions best under pressure. As the new
crisis appears, he girds for action. His adrenalin starts
to flow; his senses come to life. He feels alert, powerful,
acutely tuned, and unconquerable. Usually, his feelings
haven't deceived him. Under crisis conditions, he can
work incredible hours and accomplish superhuman
tasks. Unless he pushes himself over the edge the way
George did on his ill-advised trip, he is an awesome figure, doing the work of many and inspiring everyone
around him. At these times, he's charismatic and exciting, and when a lull occurs, he doesn't feel the same
about himself. That's one of the reasons a Burn-Out is
susceptible to the False Cures. Depending upon which
one he selects, it will supply that sensation of intensity
he likes so well, or it will deaden him to the fact that it
isn't present at the moment.

No palliative can satisfy someone on a Burn-Out
course for very long, however, because the Burn-Out
expects a payoff. If his expectation is to feel good, he'll
push harder and harder to reach that feeling. Before
long, he'll be *over*drinking, *over*eating, *over*gambling in
much the same way he had been overdoing before. The
only difference will be *what* he's doing, not *how* he's
doing it. He'll transgress exactly as he walked the
straight and narrow—with dedication and commitment,
and this behavior, combined with the denial that continues to lie beneath the surface, leads us to the ultimate
paradox: WHERE BURN-OUT EXISTS, THE SUF-
FERER UNWITTINGLY SELECTS A CURE
WHICH INTENSIFIES THE BURN-OUT, SPREAD-
ING IT FASTER AND FURTHER.

"COKE ADDS LIFE"

For several years now, cocaine has been the "in" drug among active, affluent men and women. We read about it as part of the disco scene where actors, politicians, and others we think of as highly accomplished congregate. It's offered at parties as routinely as alcohol, and in well-to-do crowds, coke spoons are given as gifts and worn around the neck as status symbols.

Cocaine, itself, has become something of a status symbol. It's expensive, so on a financial scale it rates somewhere alongside a Mercedes or a mink coat. Because it requires a connection who'll keep you supplied, it takes on overtones of successful business maneuverings. Beyond that, an elaborate system of "coke etiquette" has sprung up. There are special containers to carry it in, some of them expensive jewelry; special devices for snorting it; even special ways to snort it.

All these accouterments and adjuncts contribute to the lure of coke, but what gives it its basic appeal is its character of intensity. It's safe to say that many Burn-Outs turn to cocaine for just this reason. Since intensity is a way of life to a potential Burn-Out as well as a feeling he's accustomed to, he becomes uncomfortable when it begins to recede. As his Burn-Out increases and his energy fades, he hates the listlessness that invades him. If he's at a party one night and someone gets him to try a little coke, he'll feel a sudden rush of animation similar to what he used to feel. While he's enveloped in the glow, life takes on its old warmth, but the glow soon fades, leaving the likelihood that the individual will return for more.

Clyde's Story

Exactly that happened to Clyde one night with the result that his already burgeoning Burn-Out was swiftly accelerated. Clyde had grown up in Texas, where he attained a considerable success before he turned twenty-five. His father had died when he was a teen-ager, and although his mother had been left a small sum of money, it wasn't enough to allow the family to live the way they had lived before. There were four children, three of them sons, but somehow Clyde was the only one who felt a responsibility toward his mother. His two older brothers went on to college after they finished high school, paying their own way, but not contributing anything to the household. Clyde went to work to make it possible for his mother and sister to have a few extra comforts. While he was still in high school he worked evenings as a busboy. Then, when he graduated, he took a full-time job as a waiter. He was highly motivated, feeling proud about being "the man of the family," and before long he was making good money. What he didn't give to his mother he saved so he'd eventually be able to go into business for himself.

Clyde's "eventually" didn't take long. He was only twenty-two when his boss decided to open a second restaurant and asked Clyde if he wanted to be a partner in it. Clyde did, and he worked round the clock to make that restaurant the most popular place in town. Things couldn't have been going better. Clyde was investing his money well, and he was involved with a young woman with whom he seemed very much in love. When his mother was introduced to a widower and decided to remarry, Clyde was free to start his own life. To an observer, the script was about to have a happy ending: Young man sacrifices for mother; young man succeeds; young man lives happily ever after.

Not so, because Clyde wasn't prepared for the turnings the script had taken. He was an extremely intense young man, and he had become accustomed to functioning under pressure. As long as he was struggling to earn money, to make his business work, to support his mother and sister, he could keep going at fever pitch. Now that the pressures had disappeared, he felt depressed and discontented. He began showing many signs of a developing Burn-Out: He was irritable, restless, and cynical. He began to have quarrels with his young woman friend and to find fault with everything from his restaurant to the state of Texas. Suddenly the restaurant, which had been the pride of his life, became "that dump. You know why it's a hit? Because nobody around here knows what a good restaurant is like. I'm gonna sell out and go to New York and open a real classy joint."

Clyde did just that, or anyway, almost that. He came to New York, which he found a little overwhelming, and started to investigate the restaurant scene. Fortunately, he was a good enough businessman to refrain from doing anything rash, but every lead had to be checked out carefully, every potential partner had to be investigated. Clyde's life was centered more around delay than activity, and he was getting impatient. The success that had made him a big shot in Texas wasn't relevant to the new people he was meeting in New York, nor was the money he had accumulated as impressive as he had thought it would be. He began to yearn for some action and found it when he met Betty at a bar one night. She introduced him to the disco world and a whole crowd of "party people." Clyde began to feel alive again, especially when he found cocaine. The combination of these supercharged people and the effects of the drug brought back Clyde's sense of power. He felt warm, high, vivacious, and verbal. He was out partying every night, hitting the high spots, sometimes in the guise of checking them out as potential buys, but more often just because that's where the crowd was headed.

Clyde was dissipating his funds—and his health. He and Betty alternately used coke and slept a lot; they were either partying or unconscious. Then Clyde developed what seemed to be a chronic cold. His nose ran constantly and he was subject to bursts of sneezing, but he didn't connect it to his cocaine abuse. Not until he had two severe nosebleeds did he think of going to a doctor.

A TRIPLE BURN-OUT

Exceedingly precocious, our friend Clyde. Whatever he
did, he did it faster, harder, better than anyone around
him. In his cocaine experience, he duplicated exactly
his work experience, giving himself over so entirely to
each that he depleted himself both times. The Burn-Out
he had set in motion back in Texas came with him to
New York. In fact, leaving his home, his business, and
his friends was his first False Cure. He had come to
New York for all the wrong reasons. What he needed
when his mother announced her plans to marry was not
stimulation, but reflection. Going away for a week or so
would probably have been a good idea, but only if he
had been able to use the time and the break in routine
to take stock.

Clyde's mother's remarriage was actually the culmination of Clyde's efforts. Had he looked at it in the
right light, he'd have seen that his mother would never
have had the opportunity to meet someone if he hadn't
provided her with some leisure time. But that's not the
way he saw it. In his eyes, his position was being
usurped and he was about to become superfluous. He
didn't feel as if he had reached a goal, but rather as if
what he had accomplished had been both unnecessary
and unappreciated. Clyde was let down by the turn of
events because he had developed an image of himself as
his mother's protector. The new roles that were already
set up and waiting for him seemed tame by comparison.
Both the restaurant and the romance were proceeding
smoothly. No difficulties in either one; therefore, in
Clyde's mind, no challenges. No challenges; no intensity. No intensity; no motivation. Clyde had no recourse
but to set up new obstacles for himself in an unconscious attempt to re-create his earlier life position.

By leaving his old life behind and coming to New
York without laying any groundwork in advance, Clyde
set up larger obstacles for himself than what he had in

mind. Instead of recharging him, they overawed him, and he found himself caught in the typical dilemma of a Burn-Out: that of not being able to repudiate what he had announced he was going to do and being equally unable to function without his accustomed feelings of intensity. Enter coke, and the dilemma was solved. Clyde felt capable again and energetic. The coke made it possible for him not to notice that he was generating nothing but fruitless activity. It also enabled him not to notice that Betty was stupid and something of a parasite. It kept him supplied with a false glow that prevented him from seeing anything accurately, including the fact that he would soon be broke.

By the time Clyde got himself to the doctor, he had burned out on three fronts: He had finally been forced to relinquish his image of himself as an accomplisher; he had ruined his health; he had spent nearly all his money. If a restaurant opportunity had presented itself, Clyde would have had to let it slip by for lack of investment funds, and even if he had been able to borrow money, he'd have had to postpone a deal until after he took care of his health. He had done medical damage to the inside of his nose and required reconstructive surgery. The medical doctor made two referrals in Clyde's case—one to a surgeon, one to me.

A century before the birth of Christ, Publilius Syrus said, "There are some remedies worse than the disease," and so it turned out for Clyde. He "remedied" himself into big trouble, but luckily, he was still in his twenties and had the best part of his life before him. When he first began therapy, his progress was slow because he was intent on denying his responsibility for what he had done. Like all Burn-Outs, he had a tendency to place blame on others, but he soon realized that wasn't a productive course and dropped it. Then he veered to the other extreme, feeling ashamed for getting into such a mess and castigating himself for his stupidity. But after he got all that out of his system, he settled down to seeing how he could get his life going again. Within months, I was able to help him see he had a challenge on his hands and to remind him he was good at facing challenges. He had come through with flying colors back in Texas after his father's death. Certainly he could do as well now. He was older, more experienced, knew the restaurant business, and could point to a successful track record. Clyde found that view reassuring, and he tackled his problem eagerly. He started out once again as a waiter, and just last month, scant five years later, signed a contract for his own restaurant. His Texas girl friend is here with him in New York, and he walks fast when he has to pass a discotheque.

DESPONDENCY AND DRUGS

An aspect of Burn-Out we haven't touched upon makes the individual who is burning out particularly susceptible to the lure of drugs, and this is the despondency that often appears as the flip side of intensity. We saw it in Miriam; we saw it in Clyde. It's the letdown that comes in between crises or directly after "mission accomplished." Frequently, following a triumph, high achievers suffer periods of deep melancholia somewhat akin to the postpartum depression some women experience after giving birth. The feelings are remarkably similar: sadness, separation, sluggishness, and above all, emptiness. Performers describe it as occurring when the curtain goes down. Onstage, they've reached such a high emotional level they're completely drained when the performance ends, and since nothing flows in to fill them up again, they're on a constant teeter-totter, going back and forth between their highs and lows. We have seen flagrant examples of this in the rock world, where performers reach a superintensity during a concert. We know how widespread drug abuse is in that world, and if we examine it from a Burn-Out viewpoint, we can understand why. The music, the beat, the vibrations from the crowd, the very numbers of the crowd and the excitement those kinds of numbers can generate, the push to communicate and to be loved all unite into a giant force that sends the performer soaring. He flies high, above the sound barrier, in a rarefied, dizzying atmosphere, and when he comes down, he finds the ordinary air oppressive. Drugs mollify his pain, and so he turns to drugs.

Some people use "ups" to reproduce the high; some use "downs" to bring them forgetfulness; too many use some of one, some of the other, in a search for instant moods. Often the first step toward a drug-controlled existence comes in the form of a doctor's prescription. Depression is abundant in our society and drugs *do* help. But they never get to the root of the problem. They mask, rather than ferret out, symptoms. And people do become addicted—not just the thrill seekers among us, but also ordinary men and women who find that an amphetamine or a tranquilizer makes it easier for them to face their lives. Many individuals in a Burn-Out that could have been reversed in a relatively short time span are propelled by drugs into a very serious state.

THE INTERFACE GENERATION

As people grow older and see more of their dreams fade, they become increasingly susceptible to Burn-Out. Many of them are ruled by one or several of the denials we discussed earlier. They see themselves aging or doing less well financially than they had hoped. Their marriages or careers or sex lives are disappointing them. They feel as if they're in a rut, headed nowhere, with a lot of wasted time behind them and not a lot left in which to make up for what they've missed. All these issues are painful to confront, especially for individuals who can look back on periods of involvement and achievement. The last thing in the world they want to do is admit that things are going wrong, and so they set about curing themselves. These are the individuals who, above all others, are likely to burn themselves out further through their adopted cure. They are what I refer to as The Interface Generation, those who like Janus, the Roman god of beginnings and endings, look ever forward and back.

As you may remember, Janus was represented as having two faces, one looking to the future, one to the past, which is why our first month, January, is named for him. The segment of the population I am likening to him are those who straddle two cultures: the Old Testament, Calvinist tradition they were raised on and the new morality of the postsixties world. While we're all affected by that dichotomy to some extent, people whose formative years were over before the sixties broke loose are affected most acutely. Among other things, they don't know how to handle idleness, yet they have more time than ever on their hands. If they find something to throw themselves into, they'll become obsessive about it. The mother whose children are grown and gone and who feels useless may become an inveterate card player or soap-opera addict, actually confusing her own life with the lives of the characters on the screen. Many men in their forties and fifties dive into some physical pursuit with so little moderation that they damage their health.

When members of this group break loose, they break loose with a vengeance. I meet dozens of men and women who, after twenty or even thirty years of a doggedly monogamous marriage, are now "swinging" in every conceivable way. Countless parents who, very tentatively one evening, try pot with their children, end up outsmoking them or going on to cocaine. And as for alcohol, the consumption among this age group is notorious.

When you think about it, these contradictions are not as strange as they sound, since they're being committed by people who know only one way to do things—and that way is thoroughly. They can't discard the teachings of a lifetime, and whether they've picked "swinging" or jogging or drinking or health food, they go about it as furiously as if they were cramming for an exam. Since these individuals have been oriented to excel, they have to hold their liquor better than anyone else or jog the longest distance. The "cure" that was undertaken for pleasure or relief is shortly being governed by the work ethic!

GOING AGAINST THE ODDS

Emery's Story

Emery was a thorough man, a hard worker, and of the fourth generation in his family to go into the ministry. He had a heavy load of tradition on his shoulders, and he upheld it well. Despite the general fall-off in church attendance, Emery's congregation was large and devoted both to the church and to Emery, who discharged his duties in a nineteenth-century way. He was a learned man, and he fussed over his sermons; week after week, they were notable for their content and style.

He made it his business to visit the sick and to pay calls on all his parishioners, making the rounds at least once every year. He organized a youth group, supervised the Sunday school, involved himself in interracial activities, raised money for the church and other charitable causes. All in all, a dedicated man.

Emery's wife was a nervous, not too stimulating woman who participated in church activities when she had to, but who was happiest keeping busy with her home and children. There was no real passion between them as husband and wife, but passion was not one of the things either of them had been taught to expect from life. They were a family, their two sons and two daughters were bright and good, their responsibilities filled their time, and the years passed. Emery's one disappointment, which he never mentioned to anyone, was that he hadn't risen higher in the church hierarchy. He was well regarded by his superiors; he knew that. But somehow he was always passed over when a higher post was being filled.

As a religious man, Emery was able to assuage his disappointment by telling himself God had other plans for him; as a temporal man, he comforted himself with the knowledge that his wife preferred things to remain the same. If his prayers were for recognition, hers were to stay quietly in her home and community. Although they would never have much in the way of material possessions, they would have enough for the children's schooling and their own modest needs.

When Emery was about forty-six, his mother, who lived on the small pension allotted to a minister's widow, contracted cancer and had to undergo surgery. It was a bitter time for Emery. He loved his mother very much and was deeply affected by her suffering. He wanted her to have constant nursing care, and the best doctors, but with two children in college, he was already strapped for money. Now, the lack of promotion, which had always been a disappointment to him, began to swell into a resentment in his mind. All his devotion, his dedication, piety, and good works—what good had they been if they hadn't even made it possible for him to care for his mother properly?

Emery had no one to turn to for money nor anyone to talk things over with. His wife had never cared for his mother and wouldn't have been sympathetic to his feelings of responsibility. She would likely have pointed out to him that she was already sacrificing to keep the children in school, and Emery couldn't dispute that. As for members of his congregation—he didn't feel it would be proper for him as a minister to burden even the few he had become fairly friendly with over the years. And since he had never taken the time to develop friendships outside the congregation, he had to do what he could on his own. What he did was take out a bank loan without making the slightest provision for meeting the required monthly payments, and suddenly he found himself in trouble.

Anyone with a knowledge of Burn-Out could have predicted long before that Emery was headed for danger. For years, he had been systematically depleting his energies, never taking a break from his constant round of duties, always hoping secretly that his expected reward would materialize. He functioned in a solitary fashion, buoyed up by not one single human relationship. As his children got to college age and the pressures on him mounted, he became more mechanical and remote. His mother's illness turned out to be his breaking point, but if that hadn't served as the catalyst, something else would have. The stage was set for Emery to burn himself out. It only remained for circumstance to provide the vehicle.

When the bank began to dun Emery, he thought of going to his bishop, but was held back on two counts: First, the bishop was a cold, aloof man whom Emery found intimidating; second, he had convinced himself that the bishop was directly responsible for his plight, and he harbored a great resentment toward him. With that last avenue closed to him, Emery decided to "borrow" from the church funds. He kept a scrupulous record of the amount he was taking and prayed he would find a way to pay it back soon. But no way occurred to him, and in the meantime, the bank loan had to be paid. Not only that, the expenses for his mother's illness kept mounting. Emery was soon taking regular amounts from the collection plate and delaying deposits of contributions.

Emery was a mass of guilt, fear, and recrimination. He wasn't sleeping, and he looked terrible. Then, one evening while he was slumped in a chair in the living room brooding over his predicament, a commercial for the local racetrack came onto the television screen. "Why not?" he thought. "I'm overdue for a little luck, and I certainly don't have any other prospects." The very next day, Emery was at the track experiencing that heady phenomenon known as beginner's luck. He came home with money and a sense of power such as he hadn't experienced since he stood in the pulpit giving his very first sermon.

That night, Emery slept peacefully. He was in his office early the next day, amazing his secretary by being in high spirits for the first time in months. He made out a deposit slip to the church's account and reduced the total in his ledger book, but on the way to the bank, he began to think, "Maybe I'll be lucky again. Then I could replace *all* the money. If I didn't owe the church anything, I could go to the bishop. I've probably been judging him harshly. There must be a fund for emergencies like my mother's illness." Emery went and won again, but that wasn't all that happened to him that day. He made a friend, a real character who knew his way around the track and who gave Emery a tip that paid off big. They had a beer together and arranged to meet the day after tomorrow.

Emery was hooked. He hadn't thought of his church all day, and even when he stopped in to check his messages, his head was still spinning. Horses and races and odds were running around in his thoughts as he carefully made out a new deposit slip. This would make him almost even, and it had been so easy! He went to the bank first thing in the morning, holding out just enough for some bets the following day. Then he settled down to write his sermon for the coming Sunday and get his desk cleaned up so he would be free for his date tomorrow.

The weeks passed with Emery becoming more and more absorbed in his new pastime. He bought the racing sheets every day and, with the help of his new friend, developed an elaborate system of handicapping. His friend showed him how to keep records of his bets, complete with notes on the way particular horses performed. Emery was not only enjoying his new diversion, he was working hard at it. He bought a notebook so everything could be neatly organized, and he was as busy with it as a teen-age girl with a diary. Between his notebook and his accounting system, Emery hardly had time left over for his church. He canceled many appointments, missed meetings, and started extemporizing his sermons, using his mother's illness as an excuse when he needed one. The church's money-raising Bingo games, however, were another story. Those he never missed. They were now the source of his betting fund, and he had to guard against letting the cash receipts fall into anyone else's hands.

After a while, things began looking strange to Emery's secretary. "Who is that funny man who comes here all the time?" she asked. "Oh, he's one of the needy people the town helps," was Emery's hastily-improvised explanation. "The mayor's office asked me to work with him." Soon she was inquiring about all the long-distance calls on the phone bill, and Emery, hoping she wouldn't check and find out they had been made to racetracks, invented yet another story, this time about former congregants who were in need of counseling. Emery was becoming a walking example of Scott's famous line, "Oh, what a tangled web we weave, when first we practice to deceive!" And the web got increasingly tangled. Emery hadn't been winning consistently. In fact, he was out quite a bit of money, having taken some reckless plunges which hadn't worked out the way they were supposed to. The bills were still coming in, and the books still had to be balanced. To Emery, whose sense of morality had mysteriously vanished, these were two more challenges in his exciting game of ways and means, and he came up with an ingenious plan: He would borrow money using the church land as collateral. Not the least bit deterred by having to forge the signature of the chairman of the board of directors, he arranged for ten thousand dollars, which he lost forthwith.

Quite a cure Emery had prescribed for himself! He was eventually forced to resign from the church; his daughter and son had to leave college; his wife fell apart. The family moved, in deep shame, to lose themselves in the anonymity of New York, and Emery, nearly fifty, had to find a new way to earn a living. So seduced had he been by his gambling, he sacrificed his calling, his reputation, and his family's generations-old tradition. He also indentured himself for life by signing a paper promising to pay back the funds he had stolen.

DECEIVING OURSELVES

Emery is a stunning example of a worthwhile human being who caused his own Burn-Out by not being honest with himself. All along, he had been exhausting his energies in a fierce effort to deny his dissatisfaction with his chosen life. To live up to his religious teachings, he had to bury his anger at the church's failure to recognize him, and he had to stay in a loveless marriage. His existence had deteriorated into monotony and boredom from which he could see no escape. When he turned to gambling, he was motivated as much by his need for excitement as his need for money, but his image required a sanctimonious reason, and so Emery was willing to deceive himself.

Had anyone asked, he'd have said that, aside from his financial problems, his life was splendid; even the financial problems, according to him, were merely temporary, caused by unusual circumstances. The truth was somewhat different. Emery had been feeling the pinch of his moderate salary for a long time before his mother developed her illness. He had been longing for a new car and other comforts that he knew he would never be able to afford, and he had been experiencing twinges of envy when he saw how much his parishioners were able to do for their families.

Anything undertaken for the purpose of convincing ourselves nothing's wrong, when something is, is bound to damage us even though it's an activity that works for other people. We may be doing the same thing they are, but we're doing it for different reasons and in a far different spirit. Whereas those others are motivated by a preference for what they're doing, we're ruled by our need to turn away from something we don't want to face. They have been *drawn to* the activity by their interest in it; we have been *pushed into* it by denial. We're asking the activity to supply us with more than it was ever meant to give, and so it can never become a real cure. It's as if we were taking two aspirins to cure cancer.

Even therapy undertaken in this manner will fail to be efficacious, and yet many people turn therapy into a False Cure. They start out reading a book or going to an analyst because they sincerely want help. Something in their lives isn't working—an immediate problem or one that has haunted them for a long time. They've heard, or they feel, that it's possible to improve, and they want to. But somewhere along the way, they get diverted from their original purpose, either because they aren't seeing results fast enough or because changing requires too much effort.

That's when they turn into self-improvement "junkies." They spend hours of their week looking inward. They try every new movement, then go on to the next. They get hung up on the trappings and talk of nothing else. If you make the mistake of asking how they are, *they tell you.* It's as if they never heard the conventional wisdom that "How are you?" is a greeting, not a question. They begin to lose all spontaneity in their overwhelming desire to analyze and dissect every conversation. Instead of moving forward, they become paralyzed. They see people turn away from them, but for all their analysis, they never reach a correct conclusion. Since they've convinced themselves they've reached new levels of enlightenment, it's easy for them to rationalize that the people around them are not as sensitive or as deep as they are. Ironically, they burn themselves out in the guise of self-help.

One way to tell if you're harming rather than helping yourself with your favorite diversion is to examine how consuming it has become. Are you willing to drop everything else in its favor? Does it seem superior to the things other people have chosen to do? Does it supply the illusion of power or grandeur? Is it compensating for lesser areas of your life? Does it possess a component of danger that gives you a supercharge? That's something to be on your guard for. When danger holds a special attractiveness and becomes a compelling force in and of itself, it's safe to say that dulling and deadness have set in, and when they have, the next step is Burn-Out.

THE APPEAL OF SEX

Harriet's Story

Sex can be dangerous, as we know from current novels like *Looking for Mr. Goodbar* and items we read in the newspapers. And often that's where its appeal lies. As far back as she could remember, Harriet had always been a restless spirit. From childhood on, she had identified strongly with her successful businessman father, wanting to be like him when she grew up. Whenever he went on a business trip, he would bring her a pretty present and tell her wonderful stories about the cities he traveled to and the adventures he had. As Harriet fell asleep each night, she embellished his stories with fairy-tale images of princes and palaces, royal meetings and important conversations in which her father won everyone to his point of view. By contrast, her mother's life seemed dull and boring—insignificant, in fact. Harriet vowed, at an early age, to create a life for herself as exciting as her father's.

She was a good student in high school and easily got into a first-rate college, but soon decided she didn't like it and switched to another school in another part of the country. Then another. And still another. She contrived to go to six different schools without ever acquiring a degree. "Restless," was how she explained it. "I'm looking for something, and I'll recognize it when I find it." In her search, Harriet tried as many careers as she had tried colleges. Each time, she would seem satisfied at first, but soon her interest would wander and she would make a change. She did the same thing with men. In addition to being competent and bright, she was attractive and never lacked for dates. She had successive and overlapping affairs during her college days, but became bored with them as quickly as she did with everything else.

As bright as Harriet was, there was no way for her to know how futile her search was. She was chasing a dream, a child's fantasy world where thrills were never-ending and every moment was charged with excitement. She had raised her expectations so high, she could never reach a payoff. What she was seeking was nonstop intensity, and since even the most exhilarating pursuit soon settles into a routine, Harriet was doomed to constant disappointment.

After many letdowns, Harriet decided marriage might be the answer. She had met a handsome, flamboyant artist who was sought after by many young women, and she thought he might provide her with the stimulation she seemed to need. He didn't earn much money, but that was all right with Harriet. At the time, she had a prosperous flower shop which was providing her with quite a tidy income, and since she had always seen herself in her father's role, being the wage earner had a certain amount of appeal for her. She ended all her affairs and settled down, but not for long. Shortly after her second wedding anniversary, she abandoned both her husband and her shop.

On she went, trying and discarding people, places, and careers. Whatever she undertook achieved success because she dove into it so wholeheartedly, but as soon as it was running smoothly and making a lot of money, Harriet was off to the next thing. When she was twenty-eight, she met Mitchell, a successful lawyer of thirty-five who had never been married and therefore represented a new challenge. Harriet fell in love with Mitchell and persuaded him to give up his bachelorhood. This time, she made resolves. She was going to work at being contented, and she would take a nine-to-five job, because in her first marriage, her shop hours had caused problems. What's more, she would have children. They would certainly be a stabilizing influence!

To give Harriet her due, it's only fair to acknowledge that she stuck to her resolves for several years, far longer than she ever had before. But her restlessness couldn't be totally repressed, and one night, when she was out with some clients at a business dinner, she found herself flirting with the waiter. When the clients left, she went to a hotel with him, and that was the end of the resolves. She had never wandered off with a total stranger before, and she was quite keyed up over the daring of what she had done. She started to do crazier and crazier things. She picked up men everywhere. Once, she went into an airplane lavatory with the man who was sitting next to her; another time, she left her husband at a party and went out to their car with the husband of her closest friend. Nothing appealed to her any longer unless it was fraught with danger. She sought out either unsavory partners or risky circumstances, all the time moving closer to self-destruction.

Harriet had moments of deciding to reform. She was sure Mitchell had his suspicions about what she was doing, but she had become addicted to the excitement and couldn't cut it off. Her upbringing, her family feelings, her own sense of decency all militated against her behavior, and yet, like any junkie, she had to have her next fix. The minute some wild situation presented itself, she became sexually aroused and lost control of herself. Finally, she brought one of her pickups home on a night when Mitchell was working late, and he walked in on them.

That was the culmination of Harriet's Burn-Out. In her determination to make her childhood fantasies come true, she had killed everything good in her life and in herself. She had lost her ability to feel joy in a real accomplishment. She had lost restraint, dignity, integrity, and finally, her husband and children. Because she could never come to terms with what she considered the humdrum quality of life, Harriet tried to doctor herself with a False Cure and ended up a victim of her own prescription.

Closeness: A Real Cure

§

Before we go on to a discussion of Burn-Out in specific situations like work and relationships, let's look beyond the False Cures to a remedy that can supply some immediate relief and interrupt your developing Burn-Out right now. By this point, I hope I have persuaded you that those four D's—Disengagement, Distancing, Dulling, and Deadness—don't work. Nor do the False Cures. And the reason they don't is that they take us farther and farther away from ourselves. When we use artificial means to obscure our discomfort, whether it be pain or fear or disappointment, we allow it to fester beneath the surface and grow. We can push it away for a while, but it will surely flare up in time and return to plague us. So, then, if we can't drink or drug or gamble or disco our Burn-Out away, what can we do?

Well, since distancing doesn't work, it's logical that its opposite will. We can spare ourselves immeasurable agony and virtually turn our lives around by cultivating that rate and valuable commodity, closeness. *Just as other-directedness and distance are the allies of Burn-Out, so closeness and inner-directedness are its foes.* Where closeness exists, Burn-Out has a hard time staking out a claim. But closeness is in short supply these days and becoming scarcer all the time as living gets to be more and more fragmented. We cannot expect to experience it unless we actively seek it and work at it, and that isn't as easy as it may sound.

CLOSE TO YOU

Before we can achieve closeness with others, we have to
achieve it with ourselves. That this is often painful is
borne out by the infrequency with which we encounter
it either in ourselves or, by observation, in people we
know. Why? Why do we keep at a remove from ourselves? What is there inside us we don't want to face?
Can we really be so loathsome we have to be hidden
away, covered over, and given three coats of paint before we can be trotted out for company? Who is this
hidden being inside of us we're afraid to know? Are we
harboring a monster so terrible that, like Medusa, if we
gaze upon it, we'll be turned into stone?

It hardly seems possible, yet we behave as if it were
so. We run from ourselves every chance we get. Think
about it. When did you last spend time by yourself, with
yourself, doing something you enjoy? *With* yourself is
the important thing to check, because much of the time
we're alone we shut off our minds and feelings. We get
involved in a television program or have a couple of
drinks or fall asleep. We're not really there for ourselves in a related kind of way. We're merely alone.
Being alone *with* yourself, however, means your senses
are alive, your thoughts are keeping you company,
you're sitting in that room or going to that art gallery
with a person, not just an empty body. You're sharing
an experience *with* yourself, and you're enjoying it.

A friend of mine who lives in the Midwest has been
going bear hunting regularly for more than a dozen
years. In all that time, he has never caught a bear and
his trips to the woods have become the source of good-
humored kidding from his friends. But, as he has often
said to me, he hasn't the slightest desire to catch a
bear—he wouldn't know what to do with one if he
stumbled across it. He's there in the woods as a time-
out from city living. No phone calls, no meetings, no
television, no appointments, no city noises. His trips to

the woods are complete breaks from his overcrowded schedule, and they give him a chance to get back in touch with himself. For those hours, he's completely *with* himself—aware of the setting he's in, tuned in to the sounds and sights of the forest, conscious of his own thoughts and feelings. He may never leave the forest with a bear, but he leaves it each time with something far more important: a sense of renewal. He's given himself a chance to let old problems settle themselves before he takes on new ones. Away from his everyday, tumultuous environment, he tells me, situations that have been troubling or perplexing him take on a clarity he can never achieve at home or at his desk. He gets new insights, new perspectives that help him put his life in order.

People who burn out seldom take time for that quality of aloneness. They're caught up in a whirlwind of activities which they undertook initially because of their abundance of energy, but which have become self-generating and often as useless as they are taxing. How about your own life? Are you caught up in a round of activities you can't even remember why you started? Do you spend time with people you don't really like or whose interests are poles apart from yours? Are you less and less the deciding factor in where you go and what you do?

If you're wondering how your life slipped out of control and veered so sharply away from the direction you thought it was going to take, believe me, it was neither difficult nor unusual. In the routine of life, it's easy for this kind of thing to happen. It doesn't require a trigger as dramatic as Paul's rejection of his music. It can be, and often is, circumstantial. We get so caught up with people and job requirements and social demands that we're compelled to put our genuine interests aside. We think we'll get back to them later, but before we know it, our calendars are filled and so, instead of learning French or going fly fishing, we end up in an avalanche of business meetings and superficial social occasions.

Ask yourself: "When is the last time I set aside a few hours for a hobby or a side interest?" Then see if you can remember what was so important about all the things you *did* allot your time for. How necessary were they? How interesting and rewarding? How lasting or far-reaching? This goal you've been pursuing so relentlessly—look at it for a minute. Do you still think it's as worthwhile as you used to, or has it become an unexamined habit? Go one step further: Even if you say, "Yes, I think it's worth pursuing," does it really require so much of your time and effort? Couldn't it possibly be achieved with less? And now look at the tough question: Does your absorption in this goal or your preoccupation with your myriad activities keep you from facing other, more disturbing areas of your life?

Often, people get on treadmills like these because there's something they wish to avoid. Some area of their life is fundamentally wrong, but they either don't know how to deal with it or believe they had better not. Consequently, they establish a network of busyness with themselves at the center and the problem way off in the background just outside their range of vision. If this sounds like denial to you, you're right. Avoidance is an unconscious turning away from something, much in the manner of denial, but on a less profound level. Denial is a mechanism for coping with deep-rooted matters of an existential nature; avoidance is our way of dealing with more pragmatic situations. In the chapter "The Nonfeeling State of Burn-Out," we saw how many lives are ruled by philosophical fears—fear itself, illness, aging, death. Here, we're talking not so much about fear as about resentment; not about an abstract consideration, but about a specific circumstance that is an ongoing source of distress. Someone once said, "Life is what happens to you while you are planning your future," and avoidance is our defense against these unwanted detours and twists of fate.

AVOIDING CLOSENESS

By keeping ourselves perpetually busy, we get to avoid closeness in what, to all appearances, are legitimate ways. The wife who's busy with three teen-agers and has gone back to school to get her college degree certainly rates understanding from her husband when she's too tired for sex. It isn't that she doesn't want to, she feels just as deprived as he does, but she's got to cram for this exam! The husband who's working evenings and weekends to provide a comfortable living for his family is entitled to be excused from family outings. After all, he's not dashing off somewhere to meet another woman. He'll be right there at his desk working on his report all the time they're gone. The single daughter in the neighboring big city who works in an office all week and goes to acting class whenever she has free time can't be expected to drop everything, get on a bus, and spend time with her widowed mother. She has her future to think of.

When these kinds of things happen for a short span of time or as isolated incidents, they probably *are* legitimate, but when they become a way of life, somebody's avoiding something. The daughter may not want to face her mother's questions about why she isn't married or what kind of life she's living, always out with different men. That's fair enough, but she and her mother would have a better chance of becoming good companions for each other if the daughter would gently, but firmly, express her feelings and ask her mother to respect them. By staying away with her "busy" excuses, she's depriving them both of what could turn out to be a supportive relationship. Similarly, our busy college-student wife is creating what will eventually turn out to be an insurmountable barrier between herself and her husband. Perhaps her husband is a clumsy lover and she has never enjoyed him sexually, but she is fond of him in other ways and doesn't want to disrupt the marriage.

She's afraid that if she tells him how she feels he'll be angry and hurt. Besides, she was brought up in a home where sex was never discussed, and she finds the whole subject embarrassing. Better to avoid it, she has decided, not realizing she has picked on the most hurtful course of all.

Before women became aware that they had options, many wives lived out their entire lives with men who were no more than peripheral figures in the household. Workaholics like the one we mentioned above were good husbands in the eyes of the world. They took care of their family's material needs, they weren't abusive, they didn't come home drunk. They didn't come home much sober, either, but in those days roles were stringently divided: hers comprised the children and the home; his was work, and no one could deny that he was working. Communication and closeness weren't thought of as having great significance, so couples stayed together leading separate lives and keeping their discontents to themselves.

Carol and Carl's Story

Carol and Carl lived that way for eighteen years. When I met them, Carl was executive vice president of a major corporation, being groomed at the age of forty-two for the presidency. Without doubt, the organization couldn't have picked a better man. Carl put all his energies into his job. He was at his desk before eight in the morning, and his lights burned late into the evening. He took work home over the weekend and let his vacation time accumulate. Carol kept his food warm till he arrived home at ten or eleven, and if he had work to do on Saturdays and Sundays, she kept the children entertained and out of his way. From time to time over the years, she tried to get him to discuss what was clearly an untenable situation, but he always shrugged off her attempts with some vague answer: "Oh, it'll be different soon. As soon as this merger is locked up, I'll have lots of free time."

Carol really loved Carl and wanted to please him, but she could never find a way. She suffered from his neglect and from the terrible feeling that she was somehow at fault. Over the years, her unhappiness grew, but so, happily for her, did the women's movement. She began to read about new attitudes and new assertiveness among women. She reviewed her life and marriage, took stock of her options, and decided that she was willing to risk loneliness and financial hardship rather than stay in a hollow marriage that was robbing her of her self-respect.

One night, when Carl had finished his dinner and the children were asleep, Carol sat him down in the living room and said, very calmly, "Carl, I want a divorce." Habit is a very strong force, and Carl was in the habit of deflecting any remark of Carol's that sounded like a prelude to a talk about their relationship, so he answered by saying, "Okay, we'll discuss it next week." But Carol had expected something like that and was fully prepared. "No, Carl, we'll discuss it now. This isn't a request, and it isn't a complaint. I simply don't want to be married to you any longer, and I'd like you to move out as soon as you can find a place. I'll try to find work immediately, but I *will* need help."

Carl was nonplused. This was not like any speech Carol had ever made before. Nor did her voice sound the same. There was no pleading, no unsureness. She had thought this through and reached a decision. Carl was quiet for a few minutes, then said, "All right, Carol. I'll be out by the end of the week." For the first few months, Carl's life continued unchanged except that he went home to a compact apartment instead of a house and ate his dinners at a restaurant. He worked the same grueling hours as ever and, if anything, seemed to be even more supercharged. In telling me about it later, though, he admitted that from the time he moved out of the house, he had been different. "I was working just as long and just as hard," he told me, "but I wasn't getting things done. A couple of times, my secretary caught inconsistencies in my reports. I'd have looked like a fool if they had gone through that way."

Carl went on to recount many classic Burn-Out symptoms: his mind wandering during meetings; irritability with his staff and once or twice with clients; headaches and nagging fatigue.

Carl kept pushing himself, until one day he wasn't able to get out of bed. He called in sick, something he couldn't remember ever having done before, and stayed in his apartment for a week, not letting anyone come to visit. When he returned to work, his secretary, who had been more observant during these months than Carl had imagined, talked him into coming to see me. I had never met him before, but one glance told me he was an exhausted human being. He had dark rings under his eyes, and he couldn't seem to stop yawning. The first thing he told me was that his doctor had examined him during the week and couldn't find anything wrong, but something must be because it was out of character for him to be so tired. "I generate energy," he said. "But lately, I want to sleep all the time."

Carl's story was a chronicle of closeness starvation, and the fact that he had created it himself didn't make it easier to bear. When he and Carol met, he had been halfway through a Ph.D. program, well on his way to a professorship in economics. He wasn't serious about Carol, but after they had been seeing each other for some months, she became pregnant. Carl married her immediately, left the university, and accepted a job with his present corporation. He rose quickly in the corporate structure, and they settled into a typical middle-class way of life, complete with a house, two cars, and two more children.

I encouraged Carl to talk about his marriage, and although it was hard for him at first, once he got started, he seemed relieved to be airing his pent-up emotions. He told me he had never loved Carol, had married her out of a sense of duty, and had stayed all these years for the same reason. She was not particularly bright, he said, couldn't provide the intellectual companionship he needed, so he threw himself into his work. He was interested in matters of consequence—political and economic theory; she concerned herself with trivia—

clothes, food, the children, friends. He preferred his time at the office to his time at home and allotted it accordingly. He mentioned in passing one day that he resented Carol and his oldest son for forcing him to lose the life-style he had wanted, and yet he didn't seem to make any connection between that resentment and his stream of complaints.

After a few sessions, I persuaded Carl to take a month-long vacation. He was more than entitled to the time, and he needed it for some long-overdue introspection. He rented a cabin in the woods, loaded his car with skis and books, and set off. We talked a number of times while he was gone, and I could hear a profound change in his voice and in what he was saying. For the first time in eighteen years, Carl wasn't running from something. He was allowing his thoughts to surface without censorship and finding them less upsetting than he had expected them to be. He was happy reading the kinds of books he hadn't had time for since he left the university. With the exhilaration of skiing and the absence of pressure, both his mind and his body wound themselves down.

On impulse, at the end of the first two weeks, Carl picked up the phone and invited his son—the one he had resented all these years—to join him. They spent the last two weeks together, skiing and talking and cooking their meals. It was the first such experience they had ever shared, and they had a wonderful time. Carl came back from his vacation refreshed and chastened.

Now, two years later, he is still separated, but he and Carol have established quite a different relationship. They spend time together and have discovered they have a lot to talk about, including all the personal matters they had never aired. Carl is still successful on the job and is a better father than he ever had been before. Out from under Carl's shadow, Carol was able to venture forth. She has a part-time job during the day and is finishing the requirements for her master's degree. On the nights she has class, Carl cooks dinner for the children and spends time helping them with their homework. He is no longer afraid to leave the office at a reasonable hour, and he even takes an occasional three-day weekend.

LOOKING BACK

It is ironic that Carol and Carl have become closer in their separation than they ever were when they were living together, and yet it's understandable. If we accept that people have to be in touch with themselves before they can make contact with others, it becomes obvious that Carl's collapse and subsequent opening up swept aside the barriers he had stubbornly held in place for eighteen years. Despite his conviction that it was Carol he had been avoiding by working so hard, he had actually been avoiding himself, and this was true even at the beginning. The twenty-four-year-old Carl had done a lot of dissembling to spare himself from facing what were, to him, unacceptable issues: his own responsibility for Carol's pregnancy; his enormous anger toward her for "trapping" him; his feelings of self-pity and martyrdom. Had he been able to trust, first himself, and then Carol, he might have spared them both a great deal of unhappiness.

Trust goes hand in hand with closeness as a counterforce to Burn-Out. When you don't trust, you're on guard all the time, breeding stress that will eventually wear you out. Carl was ashamed of his feelings and didn't trust himself to express them to Carol in a moderate way. He didn't trust Carol, either, deciding unilaterally that there was no point in talking to her because she wouldn't understand. It's amazing how many people are guilty of that particular behavior pattern and how distancing it is. "Oh, I didn't ask you to the party because you wouldn't have liked the people." Or, "I didn't tell you about that because I knew it would make you angry." The individual writes a script in which he has constructed the other person's responses. Then he uses that script to condemn the person. Meanwhile, that unsuspecting other doesn't even know anything has been going on.

Making someone guilty in advance of the fact is so widespread it has given rise to dozens of funny stories. Danny Thomas became famous for one, which is about a traveling salesman who gets a flat tire on a lonely country road. He has no jack and doesn't know what to do until finally he notices a light in a farmhouse off in the distance. He starts trudging along the road, thinking furiously every step of the way, "Suppose no one's home." "Suppose they don't let me in. Farmers are notoriously suspicious." "Suppose he doesn't have a jack." "Suppose he has one and won't lend it to me." By the time he reaches the farmhouse, he has "supposed" himself into such a state that when the farmer opens the door, the salesman punches him in the mouth and yells, "Keep your lousy jack. I wouldn't use it anyway."

The story is exaggerated for effect, of course, but it captures the essence of the way we often do each other injustices. When we prejudge others' responses and don't let them speak for themselves, it's because we've created an image of them as less kind or understanding than they may actually be. We've set them up as adversaries rather than allies, never finding out what they're really like or what they'd have chosen to do in the circumstances. Sometimes we get started on this road by a family message, "Keep your thoughts to yourself, or people will take advantage of you." Sometimes we've had a parent who always answered for us. Sometimes we've been hurt. But whatever the cause, the minute we begin withholding our thoughts from others, we've begun to isolate ourselves.

I see the effects of this kind of withholding all the time. Parents, children, husbands, wives, bosses, workers all do it. They presume certain attitudes on the part of the other and refrain from sitting down to talk things over because "What good would it do, anyway?" In this way, they manage to turn a minor misunderstanding into a major rift. We read and hear all the time about the need for communication, and it seems like such an easy thing just to tell someone else how you feel, so why don't we do it? A number of reasons. For one thing, we're afraid of revealing ourselves and being laughed at or thought less of. For another, we fear that if we get close to someone else, we'll be giving that person power over us, thereby diminishing our wholeness. Paradoxically, that isn't so. The more self-contained we remain, the less chance we have for expansion and growth. Closeness is a two-way affair. We may be giving part of ourselves away, but we're also getting something back, and if we allow this give-and-take, we become enriched. Unfortunately, we have to try it to find out, but we don't because we distrust our own feelings and responses as much as we do the other person's.

If Carl had trusted himself and Carol to see each other's position compassionately, they could have discussed their circumstances with honesty rather than conventional clichés and perhaps have reached a more satisfactory resolution. Eighteen years earlier, of course, when Carol had become pregnant, there was no acceptable solution to the problem other than marriage. Abortion was illegal and dangerous; adoption was unthinkable to upstanding, middle-class families. But even so, had Carl expressed his true feelings, including his resentment and sadness over having to sacrifice his degree, Carol might happily have foregone some material comforts and put off having other children. They could have worked together to see that Carl achieved his goal and, in doing so, established some true affection for each other. Love isn't always a torrential emotion that devolves upon two people; much more often, it's an outgrowth of shared experience. Ironically, as Carl found out during the separation, Carol would have preferred to go back to school for her degree after the baby was born, but she thought she was pleasing Carl by having more children and settling into the housewife role. So it turned out that for lack of a ten-minute talk, they lived at cross purposes for eighteen years. That initial failure to communicate set the tone for their marriage. Carl set Carol up in his mind as a shallow woman who had caused him to ruin his life and, to justify that position, kept the real Carol at arm's length. To be right, he needed to make her wrong.

Although Carl convinced himself he was protecting Carol, he was basically involved with preserving his picture of himself as an honorable young man. When Carol told him she was pregnant, he responded with gallantry. When she asked him about his doctorate, he made light of it, insisting it was all the same to him whether he went to work for a corporation or a university. And although he was trying to convince himself this was true even more than he was trying to convince her, the result of his deception was that their relationship never had a chance. No relationship based on a lie ever does. It is bound to burn out as surely as the people in it.

In trying to avoid thoughts that were unacceptable to him, Carl put distance between himself and *all* his thoughts until he had no more idea of who he was than he did of who Carol was. He was far too moral a person to admit, even in his most private moments, how much he resented his oldest son, and so he threw himself into his work with an indiscriminate effort that was partially productive and partly just a function of his struggle to avoid. Without any conscious recognition on his part, Carl spent eighteen years of his life starved for closeness. Each instance of distancing affected another: He spent as little time as possible with his family; he was no more than businesslike with his associates at work; he had strayed from his college friends entirely. No one can produce constantly without replenishing his resources, and Carl was on the verge of Burn-Out long before his wife confronted him with a divorce.

BARRIERS TO CLOSENESS

If, like Carl, we've been brought up to think of certain attitudes, like not loving our parents or children, as shameful and sinful, we begin early to disguise such thoughts. If we confuse our beings with our opinions and principles, we'll be forced to defend those opinions and principles to the death, because not to do so would be to confess that it is *we* who are flawed, rather than something we just said. Moreover, if we're reluctant to accept responsibility for our actions, we'll revise reality so that it suits us and places the blame for any nonsuccess almost exclusively outside ourselves. In all these ways, we make closeness impossible. As we shrink our reality, our perception and judgment go askew. We're so wrapped up in superimposing our vision of the truth on circumstances around us, we have no room to let anyone else in. Even a helping hand is seen as an intrusion, a demand upon our energies, so we say, "Thanks, but no thanks," and continue in our aloneness and cycle of psychic depletion.

In guarding against Burn-Out, you can aid yourself immeasurably by cultivating closeness, and, of course, to do that, you must topple the barriers that keep you from it. As Carl's story points out, the most formidable of these barriers is not saying what you think. A caution here: Don't translate that to mean walking up to someone and calling him names or telling him to go to hell or worse. That's just one more distancing device. When we accuse someone or "tell someone off," we may be getting rid of some of our hostility, but we're making an enemy. The person will become defensive, and nothing will be accomplished.

By "saying what you think," I'm talking about expressing your feelings in a way that's authentic, but still engages the other's sympathies. For instance, it wouldn't have made matters better for Carl to have said something to Carol like, "You conniving bitch. You're ruining my life and my career, and I hate you." But it certainly would have been a start toward closeness if he had been able to say, "Well, Carol, we're both responsible. We'll work it out. Only I'm sad about my career. I really wanted that doctorate." He could even have added, "I'm sorry this happened," and expected her to understand.

To establish closeness, you have to be willing to take

chances. You have to trust the other person and perhaps incur some disappointments. More times than not, however, when you do put yourself on the line by opening up, you'll find the other person more co-operative than you expected. I can't stress enough how important it is to trust.

If our A No. 1 barrier to closeness is not talking, the second is not listening. Have you ever watched people in an animated discussion? Usually, at least one of them is so intent on formulating an answer to what's being said, he isn't paying the slightest bit of attention. He's dwelling on his own thoughts or feelings and holding himself aloof from the other person. He isn't listening at all. He's simply creating a forum for airing his own opinions. True listening means making a conscious effort to hear, paying close attention to what is being said. If we're serious about wanting to feel close to others, we have to give them a chance by listening on many levels: with our eyes to see what attitudes accompany the words; with our ears to hear the tone of voice; with our minds to take in their meaning; with our hearts to allow for empathy. If we do anything less, we're being unfair. We're judging superficially or with preconceived notions, and once again, we're precluding closeness.

I mentioned empathy above, and since it's a word that's often used inaccurately, I would like to expand on it for a moment. When we empathize with another, we're making a genuine effort to put ourselves in his place. We are not just extending our sympathies, although that's important, too; we're actually trying to see the situation the way he sees it. If he has just told us his father died, we're offering more than a cursory, "I am sorry." We're projecting ourselves into that bereavement, imagining how we'd feel if our father had just died. Then when we speak, we can offer true comfort.

Another barrier we have to look out for is a tendency to be defensive. If we take ourselves too seriously, we'll always be on the alert for opportunities to justify what we did or why we did it. We'll be so busy making allowances for ourselves, we won't have the time to make them for the other person. We'll be quick to accuse— either aloud, or silently, the way Carl did. Being defensive is never profitable. If you're right, you don't have to defend yourself; if you're wrong, you can't.

The most marvelous tool anyone can have in his arsenal is a sense of humor. The ability to *not* take yourself seriously, to laugh at some dumb thing you did makes life a hell of a lot less painful. There's nothing so terrible about being wrong. Alexander Pope said, "A man should never be ashamed to own he has been in the wrong, which is but saying, in other words, that he is wiser today than he was yesterday." If we could look at life that way, we'd not only be getting wiser all the time, we'd also have more fun. People who find humor in their own predicaments have a sense of proportion about life. They know that today's disaster is often tomorrow's "so what?" and they don't torture themselves and everyone around them by turning every disappointment into a tragedy. They can take criticism, admit mistakes, and allow for other points of view. Consequently, they can let people get close to them. They're not so vulnerable that they can't face life without putting fences around themselves.

To sum up: We can do a lot to save ourselves from Burn-Out by pushing our barriers aside and moving toward closeness. But first, we have to make ourselves aware of which barriers we have erected. Check yourself to see if you really trust others or if you're afraid. Then see how you are about telling. How recently have you confided something you considered crucial to someone else? Watch yourself to see if you listen. Can you really achieve empathy? Can you be responsive to another point of view even though it's at odds with your own? Can you really "be there" for another person without becoming impatient? And finally, *can* you laugh at yourself? Can you put your problems into perspective and not exaggerate them? If you're doubtful about the answers, review specific incidents and see how you handled them. Also, pay particular attention to the relationships in your life. Do they have any substance or are they all of the surface variety?

WHERE IS CLOSENESS?

Closeness is really wherever we seek it out—if we seek properly. It doesn't have to be confined to our sexual partner. In fact, contradictory as it may sound, sex is often used as a substitute for closeness. Many sexual relationships have no element of closeness or intimacy about them. In our society, people have become more comfortable undressing their bodies than their psyches. They may share a bed, but they don't share their thoughts, their hopes, their hurts. Sex is often used as a replacement for affection, rather than as an extension or an expression of it. When we hear about people meeting in a bar and going home to spend the night together, we can be sure no relatedness has been established. Group sex, sex in public places, perpetual promiscuity—none of these can be bringing people closer. Even people in monogamous situations have to be able to trust each other, listen, talk, empathize, and share in order to make contact in a significant way. Sex can serve many purposes, of course, but when it's constantly separated from affection, it doesn't give us the highest reward it's capable of and can contribute to Burn-Out.

Manuel's Story

Manuel, a handsome, well-born young man of Spanish descent, was referred to me by his medical doctor. Manuel was impotent, and I don't remember ever having seen anyone quite so embarrassed. In Manuel's case, sex didn't represent a False Cure; it was his central pursuit, the endeavor to which he was dedicated and committed. Manuel was a Don Juan of the first order, proud of his success as a Latin lover. He had always had a string of women, and he divided himself among them with scrupulous impartiality. His family had a thriving import/export business, and Manuel's duties at the firm were far from taxing.

About two years before I met him, Manuel had been married, in the best Spanish tradition, to a well-born, sheltered Spanish girl. He was fond of her and included her in his schedule, but he felt no obligation to change his habits. She undoubtedly realized that Manuel was womanizing, but she never accused him or did anything to make his life unpleasant. When he talked about her, I could see that he was more than fond of her; he had come to love her, but the very thought of love was so frightening to him, he had put it out of his mind. He was frantic to find out what was causing his impotency so it would end, but if I had said to him, "Manuel, you're in love with your wife. Your heart isn't into chasing around anymore," he would have run from my office.

Manuel's area of Burn-Out may be harder to understand than one that takes place in a career situation, but he was on a typical Burn-Out course: setting up an image of himself, not listening to his authentic feelings, rejecting closeness. Those ingredients always seem to be constant in Burn-Out individuals no matter how different their backgrounds and life-styles may be. Carl and Manuel had built different kinds of shells around themselves, but their shells served the same purpose of keeping people at a distance.

Carl avoided closeness with his wife because he held her responsible for tying him down and saddling him with responsibilities. Throughout their marriage, he did a big "might have been" number on himself. "I might have been a college professor." "I might have been married to someone brighter and more suitable." "I might have been leading a more fulfilling life." When he examined all these attitudes in the course of his therapy, he came to see them as fictions. Carol was brighter than he had been willing to give her credit for. His job was stimulating, and he was secretly proud of having climbed to the top of the ladder at a relatively young age. His life actually had all the ingredients he needed to feel fulfilled—once he allowed himself to experience that feeling.

Manuel's background had provided him with a different set of reasons for avoiding closeness, and his dynamics were different, but the end fact was the same: He was afraid of closeness, especially with his wife. He, too, had a set of secret reasons. His wife was a "good woman," a Madonna, and he was a "sinner." Sex between such a couple was wrong according to his traditions and teachings, or at least according to his interpretations of them. That was a huge barrier to Manuel, and another was forfeiting his *macho* image. No matter how domesticated the real Manuel was willing to become, his façade wasn't willing to let him. What would all the guys think if Manuel started to go home every night? He could hear the taunts already: "Manuel is no longer a man." "The great lover has turned into a henpecked mouse."

The answer to the question, "Where is Closeness?" is that it is *inside of you,* ready to work to your benefit anywhere you choose to set it in motion. If you feel lonely and isolated, you've probably set your life up that way. Look around you. You have parents or children or sisters and brothers, neighbors, co-workers, any number of people you can single out for friendship. Are you making overtures to any of them? Do you call and offer suggestions for doing things together? Or do you sit and wait for them to call you? When you speak to these people, do you concern yourself with what's going on in their lives? Do you listen—really listen—to what they have to say?

Since you are the source of your own closeness, it's worth a few minutes of your time to examine your barriers again. Do you consider yourself shy? Shy is a mammoth barrier to getting close, but perhaps if you can look at that crippling phrase, "I'm shy," in terms of "I don't trust," you'll be able to do something about it. When we say, "I'm shy," we're alluding to a state of being, akin to "I'm tall," or "I'm dark-skinned," and those are things we can't do very much about. It may even be that you've heard all your life, "Oh, Jenny [or Tommy] is shy," and you've accepted that statement as *your state of being.* But if you look at shyness in terms of not trusting other people, which is really what it comes down to, then you are free to make adjustments. "To trust" is an active verb, and we *can* change our actions. A good way to start is by analyzing what makes you tense with people, and if you come up with reasons, try to assess whether they're real or imagined. If that's difficult to determine, put your reasons to the test. Give someone the benefit of the doubt, open yourself up a little, and see what happens.

Being critical is another way we stave off closeness. When we want people to be something other than what they are, when we decide they should be smarter or more serious or more honorable or whatever it is we want them to be more of, we're making contact difficult. If we can drop those "shoulds" and get it through our heads that people *should* be just the way they are, we can allow ourselves to appreciate what's great about them and overlook the parts we don't like as much. If we wait to accumulate only models of perfection, we will wait a long time indeed. In the meantime, we will have deprived ourselves of fun and relaxation and the rewards that only shared experience can bring.

This kind of deprivation is central to the issue of Burn-Out, which is often precipitated by the individual's failure to perceive a reward as being commensurate with his efforts. That doesn't mean a handsome reward hasn't been forthcoming; it's merely that he hasn't felt it to be sufficient. And yet, we've read about vice presidencies and opening on Broadway to rave reviews. Those certainly sound sufficient, so what was lacking? If you reflect on the Burn-Outs you've read about so far in this book or the ones you may be encountering in your life, you'll notice that, in one way or another, they can all be classified as loners—private individuals reluctant to reveal themselves or let anyone invade their boundaries. So when their rewards came, they came in a vacuum, without the enrichment of genuine sharing.

Those same rewards, reveled in and gloried over with someone close, would have seemed large.

It goes without saying that the ideal setting for closeness is a love relationship, but that's something we can't all have at every stage of our lives. We *can* all have closeness and companionship, however. The potentials for them are within ourselves, and there are many human beings waiting to be approached. It will be easier to approach them if you remember we're not the only ones seeking closeness. Most people are, but they're thwarted by their barriers. You can overcome *your* barriers if you're willing to put in some effort, and I assure you it's an effort that will bring a gigantic reward in energy, enjoyment, and aliveness.

Burn-Out and Work

❦

Vera's Story

Let's imagine it's ten-thirty on a Monday morning and look in on a few hypothetical work settings. At the Subliminal Advertising Agency, a meeting is going on. The client is expected at three that afternoon for a preliminary presentation of his new campaign, and the creative team who put it together is staging a dress rehearsal for the higher echelons of management. A lot of people are at the meeting. The art director and writer, the creative director who is their immediate supervisor, the account people who serve as liaison between the agency and the client, the president and senior vice president of the agency. What they're seeing is not a surprise to them. It's the result of weeks of work and has been approved in concept form after much discussion and planning of strategies and objectives. A slogan has been agreed upon and so has the general approach to the commercials and ads. This meeting is to check out details and to smooth out any rough spots.

When the writer, a chic, late-thirtyish woman named Vera, finishes the presentation and sits down, one of the account men says, "I don't think that last script is on strategy. It talks about flavor, and our whole creative platform is built on quality." The vice president agrees and almost immediately everyone is talking at once, making suggestions for changes and offering ideas. The only silent one at the table is Vera, who's getting angrier minute by minute. While the general

144

conversation is going on, she's having a private dialogue with herself: "Damned idiots," she's thinking. "Where were they last week when I had time to do something about it? And anyway, what the hell do they know? Flavor is as much a quality story as anything else. They're ruining my script for no reason at all, the illiterates."

By the time her creative director turns to her to ask how she feels about what is actually a minuscule change, Vera has progressed from angry to furious to livid. "Are you okay, Vera?" he asks, solicitously. She doesn't say anything, but her face answers for her, and he tries to be conciliatory. "Do you think you can revise the script by this afternoon? I'll be glad to help." "You've been a lot of help so far," Vera snaps at him and storms out of the room, leaving everyone at the table upset and uncomfortable.

Vincent's Story

At the same time, in a classroom across town, Vincent, an art teacher who has shown great promise as a budding educator and who used to receive glowing reports from his principal, sits at his desk reading a book while his seventh-grade class gets more and more unruly. Vincent has been having a hard time lately getting out of bed in the morning to face another day of teaching, so some mornings he smokes a joint or takes a tranquilizer before he leaves the house. Today, his morning fortification seems to have affected him more than usual, and although he's aware the class has gotten out of hand, it all seems rather far away and not worth bothering about.

Fortunately for Vincent, however, his friend Howard, who teaches across the hall, thinks it's worth bothering about and comes into the classroom to restore order and shake Vincent out of his lethargy. Howard has been concerned about Vincent for some time now, and when the bell rings, he suggests that they spend their lunch hour together to talk things over. Vincent is reluctant. "Thanks, Howie, but there's nothing to talk about. Listen, I appreciate your coming in. Don't know what's wrong with me this morning. Guess I'm coming down with something."

"It's not just this morning, Vin," Howie answers, "you're in a funk, and I'd like to help you get out of it. I'm sure if we talk, you'll feel better."

"It's not me you oughta be talking to," Vincent answers angrily. "Try talking to these animals. I must have been crazy to think I could teach them something about art. I might as well be training cripples for the Olympics." But Howard won't take "no" for an answer, and Vincent finally agrees, realizing that despite his protests, it will be a relief to talk about the way he feels.

Molly's Story

At precisely ten-thirty that same Monday morning, a nurse in the intensive-care unit of a large hospital watches a patient die. For Molly, who's been head of this ward for five years, this should be a routine occurrence—"all in a day's work"—but somehow it isn't. She had become fond of this patient and been touched by her suffering. She had watched the family come day after day to offer what comfort they could, had seen their despondency increase as the weeks passed, and now she feels as if she has lost someone close. Before she goes to call in other staff members, she walks over to the window and stands there, weeping a little, a stream of angry thoughts rushing through her mind: "What the devil is it all for? You worry and you try and you rush in a dozen times a day and you care about them and it doesn't do a damn bit of good."

She becomes aware of footsteps, and she turns. The patient's doctor has come into the room. He and Molly have worked together for years in a relationship of mutual respect. She has always considered him the best doctor on the hospital staff; similarly, he has considered her the best nurse—professional, efficient, conscientious, and meticulous. He's shocked to hear Molly's voice, trembling with anger, saying to him, "Where were you? If you had made it your business to get here sooner, we might have saved her." Even as she says it, Molly knows it isn't true, but she can't seem to stop. "You could have done something—given her something. She was so brave. But what do you care? They're all the same to you. Just a bunch of cases, that's all."

The doctor is not only shocked, he's hurt. How could Molly, of all people, accuse him of being unfeeling? Better than anyone, she knows the hours he puts in, the fights he's always having with the administration for better patient care. Without stopping to consider why Molly is so overwrought, he retreats into his most aloof professional manner and says coldly to her, "Nurse, I'll see you in my office in half an hour."

Benjamin's Story

This Monday morning seems to be bad everywhere. At an alcoholic clinic noted for its high rehabilitation results, Benjamin, a counselor, and his patient, Max, are having their weekly session. Max, like most alcoholics, is a difficult patient, dependent, passive, needy, and worst of all, regressive. Every time he seems to be making progress and Ben feels, "At last we're getting somewhere," Max stops in at a bar or has "one too many" at a party. This, of course, is par for the course with alcoholics and why Max is in treatment in the first place, but Ben has come to think of it as deliberate and directed against himself. He's disgusted with Max and has come closer and closer to showing it.

Today, Max has arrived half an hour late for his appointment, and Ben could tell the minute Max walked in that he had been on a binge over the weekend. "Sorry I'm late," Max says sheepishly as he sits down. "I overslept." Ordinarily, Ben would say something noncommittal and wait for Max to get around to what's been going on with him, but not this morning. This morning, the counselor in Ben has vanished and a cynical, wisecracking side of him has taken over. "Should

have come straight from the bar. You could have slept
in the waiting room," he quips.

Max sits there silent, his eyes averted from Ben, who
keeps on badgering him. "Nothing to tell me today,
huh? Well, we don't have much time left, anyway.
Maybe you ought to go out and get drunk again.
You're good at that. In fact, it's what you do best."
Max doesn't say another word during the few minutes
left to his hour even when Ben, remembering his role,
takes himself in hand and asks how things are at home.
"C'mon, Max," he adds, "I was only kidding around."
But it's too late. Max won't be back and Ben knows it.

EXPLORING THE BURN-OUT

We've just witnessed four people at that critical stage of
Burn-Out where their self-control has snapped. Nothing
extraordinary happened to any of them that morning,
but they had all been systematically depleting their resources for a long time, and so nothing much was required. The agitation that had been building up inside
them for months and that they had been struggling to
contain had grown too large to repress. All their pent-
up resentments had burst forth in displays that were
completely out of character, but that revealed classic
Burn-Out reactions: cynicism, heightened irritability,
mistrust of others, paranoia, and grandiosity.

In each case, exhaustion played a major role. Vera,
Molly, Vincent, and Ben were all overworked and had
been adding to their burdens by keeping their feelings
bottled up. The more cranky and ill-tempered that
"real" person inside of them became, the harder their
images worked at remaining co-operative, good-
humored, and capable. That was what they had always
been and how they thought of themselves. But they
were paying a huge price in inner harmony for their
dissembling. Their separation from themselves was such
that they were as startled by their outbursts as the people around them were. Later, in discussing the inci-

dents, they all described similar feelings: "It was as though I were watching somebody else. I couldn't believe I was acting that way." What really shook them up was the intensity of their behavior and its disproportion to the precipitating events. During their subsequent therapy, they all acknowledged that their outbursts had been brewing for a long time, but they still couldn't envision themselves as having acted so inappropriately.

Since Burn-Out, more often than not, is precipitated by a work situation, we can learn a lot by looking more deeply into these cases. As we do, try to notice any similarities between what we're discussing and your own situation. When something comes up that seems parallel—whether it has to do with your feelings, your physical condition, or the conditions of your job—jot it down. Your notes will come in handy a little later as we examine both the factors that combine to create Burn-Out and ways of combating them. Note particularly how the structure of work in our current society sets people up for disappointment and frustration and keep in mind that, while we can't always change the structure, we can do a lot about the way we react to it.

Look at the difference between Vincent and Howard. After all, they were teaching in the same school. They both had to contend with the same problems, the same children, the same working conditions. And yet Vincent was burning out while Howard, who had been at the school two years longer, was enjoying his job. If we look at their attitudes, we can see why.

Whereas Howard accepted his role—that of a teacher doing a job—and was content with modest victories, Vincent saw himself as a crusader out to improve the world. He had been an outstanding student and, with a B.A. in fine arts and a master's in education, had been offered positions in several upper-middle-class suburban schools. He had turned all of them down, preferring to work in a disadvantaged inner-city neighborhood, believing that his approach to art would open up new horizons for the underprivileged students he would find there. He expected these youngsters to dip into self-expression the way

Pandora had dipped into her box. Their lessons with him were going to counteract all the years of deprivation they had undergone, and while he didn't go so far as to think he could turn out dozens of Picassos, he had a vivid picture of grateful young men and women returning to thank him for steering them away from lives of lassitude and crime.

Both Vincent's parents were college professors, and from the time he was small, he had seen students come to the house, proud to be invited and eager to hear anything his parents had to say. This had impressed Vincent, and he left for college steeped in the message, "In our family, we help young people find richer, fuller lives."

Vincent's dream was to go even further than his parents had. They dealt with the middle class; he would offer himself to the poor. What he didn't take into consideration and had no way of ascertaining in advance was that he was not simply going one step further. He was going into another world. His students were as unprepared for him and his ideals as if he had appeared from Mars. Not only didn't they share his enthusiasm for art, they were also self-conscious about expressing themselves creatively, and they reacted to him sullenly. They were suspicious of his friendly, contemporary approach, and he found himself treating them with a measure of respect far greater than that with which they treated him.

Nor were the children Vincent's only disappointment. The school was old, ugly, and in disrepair—a far cry from the placid campus where his mother and father taught. The rules and regulations were endless. There were lesson plans to devise and follow, endless forms to fill out, student evaluations that had to be turned in monthly. Vincent found all of this unnecessary and annoying and, instead of doing it routinely as the other teachers did, kept putting it off until he was late and had to struggle with piles of papers. He was also horrified to find the art supplies hopelessly inadequate, but since he hated to complain, he bought them with his own money. Later, when he discovered that the kids were stealing the supplies for barter in the neighborhood, he felt betrayed. How could they be so unappreciative? How could they be so dishonest when he had been so straightforward in his dealings with them?

Through all this, Vincent refused to lower his standards or accommodate to the realities. He kept plugging away with the same surface zeal, keeping his gripes to himself, but anyone who knew him as well as Howie did could sense he was not the same Vincent. Inside, frustration and anger were mounting. His energy level dropped way down. His sense of humor had vanished. When a group of teachers got together in the lounge or cafeteria and began to joke about the system, Vincent neither laughed nor participated. Either he'd retreat into the book he always seemed to be carrying these days, or he'd put a stop to the fun with a gruff, "What's so funny about that?"

This attitude was indicative of another difference between Vincent and Howard. One of Howard's built-in antidotes to Burn-Out was that he was a participator. Vincent was a loner. While Howard got a lot of pressure out of his system in gripe sessions with the rest of the staff, Vincent kept everything bottled up. He had been taught to do things by himself, had always been told that going to others was a sign of weakness, and so he deprived himself of a positive support system that could have strengthened him. Howard was free from such restrictions and eagerly took advantage of all the help he could get.

Gradually, despite Vincent's best efforts to control himself, the effects of his one-sided relationship with his students began to show. He began to dislike the children and found himself belittling their feeble attempts to draw. On days when he was particularly irritated, he would make sarcastic comments: "You call that a woman, Man? Looks like a grizzly bear to me." Of course, that only made matters worse and Vincent knew it, but he couldn't seem to keep himself on a consistent course. One day, he'd be pleasant; the next day, he'd do an about-face. He would have resigned if the idea of quitting hadn't made him feel like such a failure. Besides, teaching jobs were difficult to find, and he had lost sight of the fact that there were other things he could do with his art talents. Getting out of bed in the morning became his hardest act of the day, and the morning joint was becoming more of a ritual.

When he and Howie went out to lunch that Monday, Vincent was finally willing to acknowledge he was in trouble and to listen to what Howie had to say. He was shocked to find that Howard had come to teaching with the same goals he had brought to it; in his self-absorption, he had assumed he was the only high-minded person in the school. "We all go through this, Vin," Howard explained. "Only some of us are easier on ourselves. We learn to be pleased with one or two successes a year. And if you look back, you'll come up with more than most. Think of the Jackson kid. And Alicia. And Nick."

Gently, Howard pointed out that Vincent's attitude was not only self-defeating, it was also arrogant. "Don't you realize you've been playing God? You decided all by yourself what would be best for those kids. The rest of us take our cues from them." Arrogant! That word got to Vincent. "Gee, Howie, I never thought of it that way before. Is that what I'm being with those kids?" "Well, you sure aren't being humble," Howie said with a smile. "Vin, I'll make a deal with you. I know your evaluations aren't done, and I know you're in no state to do them. I'll come over a couple of evenings and help you get them out of the way. But you've got to promise me you'll go for therapy. You've got to start getting some perspective about this job."

They shook hands on it, which is how Vincent ended up in my office. We had a lot to do to counteract his Burn-Out, but Howard had gotten him off to a good start by offering him just the right balance of sympathy and reproach. Howard was firm without being unkind and was sympathetic enough to realize that Vincent needed tangible support more than he needed advice. Two things Howard did are very significant and should be kept in mind if you're dealing with a Burn-Out.

First, he lightened Vincent's burden by helping him get through the paperwork, which Vincent, in his despondent, edgy state, could not have tackled alone. Second, he named several students Vincent had influenced positively over the years and reminded him that if he stopped dwelling on negatives, he would see that these successes amply offset the failures. It's always important to help a Burn-Out remember his successes, because it's a given that his failures are plaguing him.

BURN-OUT AND THE HELPING PROFESSIONS

It's not easy for the men and women in the helping professions to discount a failure. Nor can they always see that there's a long distance between failing and not having a success. In all helping situations, there are many circumstances beyond the helper's control. Vincent was not dealing with his students in a vacuum. He had them for a few hours a week; the rest of the time, they were subjected to influences on the streets and in their homes more constant and powerful than what Vincent could bring to bear. So, too, with Ben and Molly. Not every alcoholic can be saved and certainly not every medical patient. But it's easy to lose one's objectivity when one is constantly surrounded by suffering.

Helpers are exposed almost exclusively to the negative sides of the people they work with. Patients don't come for counseling to talk about the positive parts of their lives. Those parts they're coping with. They come to discuss their problems. If they have a great sense of humor or profound thoughts about politics, the therapist seldom knows about it. In his role, he hears the worries and the complaints, the excuses and the "I can'ts." Had Ben and Max met outside the clinic, Ben would have seen a much more rounded picture of Max and would probably have noticed a lot of good in him. As it was, however, Ben saw only a hostile drunk who was dumping on him. Multiply this by dozens of patients each week, add the less-than-satisfactory working conditions, and you can begin to see why Ben was burning out.

That segment of the population which is attracted to the helping professions is particularly sensitive to feelings and behavior, and unless an individual has strong compensating factors in his life, he can fall victim to the constant onslaught of despair his patients bring him. The Bens of this world have a large component of social-mindedness and a desire to help. They bring much dedication and commitment to their jobs, but little preparation for the frustrations they're destined to face.

We know Burn-Out stems from a struggle to preserve something the person perceives as worthwhile, whether it be a goal, an ideal, or a contribution to society. What militates against the individual in the helping professions is that he's fighting a battle on at least three fronts: the pressures of society, the needs of the people he's serving, and his own personality traits.

The work of the helping professions is taxing and tough. Rewards are often few and not highly visible. Pressures are constant. New situations calling for ingenuity as well as diligence crop up all the time. The helper has come to his profession with visions of a supportive institution peopled with wise superiors and cooperative patients, students, or clients. He has contemplated results and tangible proof of his ability to create a difference in people's lives. What he finds instead is red tape, harried administrators, intractable cases. No one has prepared him for this. No one comes forward to ameliorate his feelings of inadequacy, and this is where his own psychological make-up comes into play. If the worker has been looking for the kind of personal fulfillment he should be finding elsewhere, he will quickly begin to burn out.

Not everyone is lucky enough to have a Howard in his life. All too often, no one is watching. In the busy world of hospitals, clinics, agencies, and schools, everyone is caught up in his own struggle. There isn't time for analysis of fellow workers or praise for a job well done. Consequently, many valuable individuals are lost. If you are in the helping professions, you must be aware of your own search for compensation and be able to ask yourself the right questions. Have you entered your profession to compensate for inadequate parenting? Do you have an undue need for power? Is your own life unsatisfactory? Are you seeking to work out your own problems through your clients? Are you looking for more from your clients or your students than they are able to give? Beyond looking at yourself, take a look at society and its values. Are you endeavoring to live up to some standard set by the community? Have you fallen victim to a philosophy in which there are no provisions for failure? Have you, moreover, neglected to re-examine the concepts of failure and success that have been imposed upon you? Are you running a childhood message through your head?

Since no one's life is static and we all go through good periods as well as bad, there are times when our needs are greater than at other times. It's very important to watch out for these periodic fluctuations and to be on guard against a lessening of our coping abilities. Our systems have to maintain some balance between what they're taking in and what they're putting out. When we're under stress in our personal lives, we have less tolerance for the stresses of work, and unless we make concessions to the increased pressure that is being put on us, things can get out of hand quickly. Remember that stress can be generated by positive as well as negative changes. Adjusting our nutritional habits, and losing ten or twenty pounds, can affect our mood. So can the completion of a burdensome task, even if it has had a successful result. Then, of course, there are the negatives that we have to pay particular attention to: a recent illness, a love affair gone wrong, a death in the family, the move of an agency, financial setbacks, the leaving of a supportive colleague.

Ben was in one of those bad periods when we looked in on him. Ordinarily, he was one of the mainstays of his agency, able to handle a heavy case load as well as the inconveniences of the agency's physical plant. Like most organizations that depend on government funds, Ben's agency was operating on a shoestring. The building needed a coat of paint, the men's room was in disrepair, counselors shared offices and a telephone that was down the hall. It was not a cheerful place to go to every day, but normally it didn't bother Ben. For the past year, however, his home life had been deteriorating. His wife had gone back to work after four years of staying home, and Ben felt threatened and disrupted. Although she had never complained about his relatively low income, Ben interpreted her decision to take a job as a criticism of his earning power. She had been a crackerjack legal secretary before their son was born, and it didn't help Ben's ego that she had been offered a salary nearly as high as his. He was also disturbed about putting their son into a nursery school, even though the school was a good one and the boy seemed to enjoy it. Worst of all, the routine of their lives had changed. If his wife was detained at work, she expected him to give their son dinner and help prepare theirs. On weekends there were household chores which Ben had to share; previously, his wife had done them during the week.

In his head, Ben approved of all this. Certainly he was no male chauvinist. But in practice, it was a difficult adjustment, especially since the last thing he'd have done was confess his feelings to his wife. What he did, instead, was gripe about his work. Suddenly he was noticing the chipped paint and the dripping faucets. He began to resent not having a telephone at his left hand and having to share an office. He complained about the chairs in the room where he saw his patients—and about the patients themselves. After a few months, the change in him was noticeable, and his supervisor called him in for a talk. "What's wrong, Ben?" he asked. "You've been having a lot of cancellations lately." Ben shrugged. "Oh, everybody has cancellations. You know how these drinkers are." The supervisor kept trying. "Ben, everybody hasn't had cancellations. Just you. Besides, I've been getting the impression you're not yourself lately. Is everything all right at home?" "Of course everything's all right at home. Look, I'll check into those cancellations. Okay? And meanwhile, why don't you do something about the chairs in those counseling rooms? Maybe they're the reason patients are staying away."

That was the first meeting with the supervisor. At their second talk, Ben was much angrier and lashed out against his patients. "What d'ya expect from the bums we get around here? Bottom of the barrel, that's what they are. Use this place as a hangout. You think they're motivated to get better? Bunch of con artists, the lot of them." The supervisor tried to reason with Ben, pointing out to him that their referrals were still coming from the same place, that if anything, the clientele were younger and more amenable to treatment. When Ben stuck to his guns and insisted the cancellations had nothing to do with him, the supervisor had to be more direct. "You've been on this job a long time, Ben. Maybe it's getting to you. I think you should do something else in the agency for a while."

The supervisor's suggestion was a good one and one I highly recommend for a burning-out worker, but—and this is an important but—it must be presented in a nonpunitive manner. Someone who's burning out has more than a touch of paranoia and is apt to interpret such a measure as one more sign that he's not appreciated and probably never has been. In Ben's particular case, it came at a bad time, since his home situation was already causing him to suffer from self-doubt. He might have been spared a lot of agonizing if the agency had a routine policy of rotation, but because of its severe understaffing, this had never been feasible.

A FEW PRECAUTIONS

Even when life is going along smoothly, people in the helping professions have to watch out for pitfalls. Molly wasn't going through any particular crisis at the time of her Burn-Out, but, like Ben, she had been doing the same difficult work for too long. In an intensive-care unit where the suffering is concentrated and almost unrelieved, a nurse is required to be a calming influence, objective and professional no matter what she's feeling inside. While the doctors come and go, the nurse is on duty for eight crisis-filled hours. In the intensive-care unit, she's overseeing the hospital's most serious cases in a setting that creates no balance between suffering and recovery, since as soon as people are less than critical, they're moved to another floor. A person would have to be superhuman to be impervious to such an atmosphere. In the course of a week, a nurse like Molly sees more misery than most people see in a lifetime, and when you multiply those weeks into years, it's obvious that precautions must be taken.

In a busy hospital where everyone including the administrators are always under pressure, what is often taken, instead, is the path of least resistance. Because the Mollys of this world keep things running smoothly and make everyone's burden lighter, they are seldom given any relief.

If you are in one of these taxing professions, you have to learn to be on the lookout for your own symptoms. Watch yourself for tiredness before it becomes extreme exhaustion. Don't fall into the trap of considering yourself a superbeing who doesn't require rest. Everyone requires rest, and your need for it isn't a sign of weakness. Pay attention to physical symptoms like colds or headaches or nagging pains in the back. Your physical system is a good barometer of whether or not you're overdoing, and a day off early may save you weeks later.

Molly had been wearing herself out for months. She had become so intensely involved in trying to relieve the suffering on her ward, she had forgotten that she, too, was a human being with needs. What Molly had done was lose her objectivity, which is the single biggest danger a person in the helping professions faces. There's a fine line between dedication and overdedication, commitment and overcommitment, and the helper has to be on guard against crossing it. A positive involvement implies mature concern and sumpathy while retaining a life of one's own. It means an interest, even an absorption, in someone or something, but with some emotional detachment. When you become overinvolved, you put yourself into an emotional or intellectual bondage to a particular ideal or course of action. And that's when the trouble starts.

It's hard, when you're caught up in something, to watch yourself, yet only you can judge the changes within yourself. You must monitor yourself constantly, not just for physical symptoms, but also for shifts in attitude. Whereas you once felt charismatic and capable, do you now doubt your own powers? Are you disappointed in yourself because you haven't been performing miracles? Do you feel a diminishment of your leadership qualities? Are you resenting the pressures you feel your patients and co-workers are putting on you?

People who choose to go into the relatively low-paying helping professions usually have a sense of mission. They are compassionate and caring, which makes them especially vulnerable to the excessive demands that are made on them. The population they're dealing with is in extreme need. It is composed of troubled or deprived human beings with a void so huge it is almost impossible to fill it. These people take, drain, demand. They require continual giving and assume an endless supply on the part of the helper. Unless the worker remains aware of his limitations as a human being, he will begin to burn out. And once he does, the conditions of the job will speed him on his way. If, as is common, the rest of the staff is harried and busy, they can't be counted on to supply an occasional compliment or the kind of morale boosting that could help. As we saw with Molly and with Ben, the happy endings that could fortify don't occur very often.

One of the ways you can protect yourself from Burn-Out is to acknowledge your feelings. If you find the repetition of tasks monotonous and boring, speak to your supervisor and arrange for a rotation of chores. Take a minute in the course of a day to pat someone else on the back. Perhaps it will become a reciprocal pastime. Cultivate friendships on the staff, so that you can exchange viewpoints and offer each other relief. Talk about your frustrations and disappointments, not in a dumping, whining way, but as an opening for others to participate and get some of their burdens off their chests. Busy as the agency, school, or hospital is, time must be made for camaraderie. If it isn't, many valuable people will be lost.

On a personal level again, watch for signs of a growing rigidity on your part. That's a sure sign trouble's brewing. Increasing negativity and cynicism are other signs. Keep track of changes in your life and of stress situations you may be undergoing. Above all, never lose sight of the fact that you, as a human being, are more important than the task, no matter how crucial the task may be.

Although the helping professions are not the only ones where Burn-Out flourishes, they have their own set of built-in problems that require particular caution. There are already too few helpers in proportion to the people seeking help, so if you are in one of these professions, you are not expendable. You can, however, be spared for a vacation, and if you suspect that you are beginning to burn out, you should seriously consider taking one. Someone else can fill in for you for a few days. And if you haven't any extra money to spend at the moment, don't use that as an excuse. Even if you have to stay home, a change of routine will do you a world of good. But use it to get your sense of balance back. Cut your job down to size. Emphasize other areas of your life to give yourself a better-rounded foundation. Feel entitled to a little pampering, because you are. A good many people depend on you. You are responsible and hard-working, and you deserve an occasional reward.

Burn-Out and Work II

❧

I've dwelt on the helping professions at some length because they delineate so sharply the forces that combine to sabotage the striver, but they aren't the only career pursuits fraught with disappointment and stress. Every occupation today seems to have built-in booby traps for the individual. As human beings, we function best in small groups where work is conducted on a personal basis and where everyone has an over-all view of what is going on. When we were largely an agricultural nation, each farmer worked his "forty acres," turned over the land, planted, watered, weeded, harvested, and drove his crops to market with justifiable pride. He—and only he—was responsible for those crops, and that was a good feeling. Those crops were not an abstraction to him: He had started them, nursed them, and brought them to fruition.

Similarly, when a few people work together in a cohesive atmosphere, exchanging information and ideas, they all derive satisfaction from seeing the result of their joint efforts. *A* has helped *B*, and *C* was able to participate because he knew what the first two were trying to accomplish. Today, however, the small entrepreneur is becoming an endangered species, fighting for his life against the more powerful resources of the large corporations. Once upon a time, it was the dream of most Americans to "be their own boss"; now, with the high cost of technology required to do business, consolidation is the order of the day.

THE SMALL ENTREPRENEUR

Those who do persevere at running businesses of their own find themselves beset with problems. To stay in business, their prices must be competitive with what the giants are charging, yet their purchasing power is so much smaller, they usually have to pay far more for goods and supplies. Sometimes they're forced to sacrifice quality, either of workmanship or materials, in order to compete, and this touches off a conflict between their drive to succeed and their value systems.

A former patient of mine, a Scandinavian of impeccable standards, was propelled into a Burn-Out by this very kind of conflict. He had been a master electrician in Europe, and when he acquired a license here, he set about his craft with the same meticulous attention to detail he had been taught in his apprenticeship. Soon he had a reputation for being that rarest of creatures—a craftsman who charged reasonable prices—and he was in constant demand. As the calls for his services multiplied, he hired a staff of electricians, assuming they would turn out the caliber of work he was accustomed to. He felt a real pride in seeing his business grow, but his disillusionment was not long in coming. The men were not doing the kind of work he expected, and for the first time in his life, he was getting complaints from his customers. He was devastated, and to add to his mortification, the union demands for hourly pay compelled him to raise his rates. So there he was, an ethical man, charging higher prices for what he rightly considered shoddy work.

To a man of conscience, this kind of struggle becomes intolerable after a while, and it is only one of many that have to be faced. I have heard tales of distress about being too small a force to get credit from banks and having to go to usurious—sometimes illegal—money sources. Entrepreneurs have told me how troubled they are over violating government regulations, yet they feel they have no recourse because of the expense involved in compliance. Payoffs and kickbacks are frequently demanded for equipment and services, and I've listened more than once to shamefaced confessions of otherwise honorable men and women dealing in stolen goods, a practice so widespread that a tradesman who refrains is unable to keep his prices competitive. When, out of desperation, a merchant finally succumbs to buying from criminal sources, he soon finds himself falsifying his income-tax return, since he has no plausible way to explain where the merchandise came from. These unsavory business practices are anathema to someone with a background of morality and honorability, but with survival—both his own and his family's—at stake, he will often compromise his ethical standards. Once he does, he lives in constant conflict, which in turn creates constant stress and opens the door to Burn-Out.

THE LARGE ORGANIZATION

Statistics (Dun & Bradstreet) show that four out of five small businesses fail within five years of being started, and even our capsulized chronicle of problems makes it easy to see why. Unfortunately, that leaves most of us working for giant institutions which are at the opposite extreme from our farmer plowing his forty acres. If we do get to plant a seed within these mammoth structures, we scarcely ever find out if it has blossomed into a flower. And if, by some chance, we stumble across the result, so many hands will have played a part along the way that we can scarcely claim credit for it as our own.

Both government and private corporations have become so big, people feel dwarfed and inconsequential within their framework. Far from working in an autonomous or intimate situation, employees have become microscopic dots in establishments huge enough to be layered and departmentalized, spreading out over many floors of a building, then spilling over into other buildings. Often, two departments that work closely with each other are so distant their members have contact only on the telephone. No wonder people feel dwarfed and inconsequential! They work with faceless colleagues on splintered projects of which they have never been given a comprehensive view. Their sense of purpose vanishes, and the work becomes less and less meaningful.

It is one thing to be a cog in a wheel, but quite another not to know where the wheel is going. Without a sense of destination or completion, it is impossible for workers to feel pride or even interest in their work. Since they don't know exactly how they fit into the picture, the tasks they perform come to seem arbitrary, and in short order the distancing process takes over. What happens is that the worker, already dejected by the remoteness of the end product, shields himself by moving farther and farther away from the job until his attitude deteriorates into "I don't care," and his actions become mechanical. This is equally true on an assembly line where someone hammers out hubcaps day after day but never sees a finished automobile, and in an office where someone is asked to assemble facts and figures but is never told what they will be used for.

The more competent the worker, the more he suffers from this fractionalization. As his creativity is stifled, his frustration mounts. He thinks back to the glowing job description he heard in the personnel director's office when he was being interviewed, and wonders how it translated itself into such a morass of memo writing, record keeping, and time-wasting meetings. He despairs of ever making progress in a company where he never sees the decisionmakers and where every innovative idea he presents seems to die in the memo stage. Although he was originally encouraged to suggest new projects and procedures, he has to submit his suggestions to his department head, and they seem to die there without reaching the channels that could implement them. A worker caught in such a bind is a likely candidate for a functional Burn-Out, by which I mean a Burn-Out generated by the system itself.

THE NATURE OF THE SYSTEM

The larger the organization becomes, the more layers it seems to acquire, with every layer needing to justify its existence. In such a structure, the emphasis shifts from the work itself to the outward signs of work. If we return for a minute to our teacher, Vincent, we'll recall how he was as much oppressed by the tons of paperwork he was required to turn in as he was by the children's failure to respond to him. And indeed, it comes as a shock to most teachers to find lesson plans deemed more important than lessons; to find themselves rated on the reports they turn in rather than the job they do in the classroom. Similarly, it disturbs people in business to find themselves spending time on everything but what they were hired to do.

Since every office has its share of insecure people (not to mention incompetent ones), much of the memo writing originates so someone can prove to someone else he did something that day. Department heads encourage their subordinates to hold multiple meetings and circulate the minutes in the hope their departments will look productive and busy. In many organizations, the process degenerates into that oft-joked-about syndrome known as PYA (Protect Your Ass), but to someone who is neither incompetent nor insecure, it isn't amusing. In such a structure, the competent individual finds himself in a no-win situation. If he ignores the system and spends his time quietly doing his work, he'll be exposing himself to two dangers: being considered unco-operative, and not having a record of his activities when he comes up for review. If, on the other hand, he goes along with what's expected of him, he's apt to lose his relatedness to his work.

To be engaged day after day in something that seems essentially meaningless is a guaranteed route to Burn-Out, especially to someone with aspirations. But let's suppose the job does have meaning and you are good

enough at it to win yourself some recognition. Does that
mean you've beaten the system and there is smooth sail-
ing ahead? Not necessarily. It may mean you will become a sitting duck for that strategy known as the Peter
Principle, a phenomenon isolated by Dr. Laurence Peter and Raymond Hull. According to their observations, "In a hierarchy every employee tends to rise to
his level of incompetence," and if we extend that definition by adding the phrase, "or something he does not
wish to be doing," we will have covered the possibilities
of where a job well done may lead.

Suppose for a moment you are a computer program-
mer in a large company. You studied computers because you're a technology nut and you genuinely enjoy
working with the machines. You do a great job for
which you're rated highly every review period. Eventually, as the computer department grows, someone is
needed to manage it, and since your record is outstanding, the position is offered to you. Well, for one thing,
you may have no managerial skills, which means, as
Dr. Peter has pointed out, you will be on the verge of
reaching your level of incompetence. But even worse
than that, you may not *want* to be a manager, because
you know being a manager has to do with records and
reports and people and problems, and you may never
get near a computer again.

You can, of course, refuse the promotion, but if you
do, you'll have limited both your salary potential and
your standing in the company. According to the rules of
the hierarchy, your current job has a ceiling, and if you
want to rise, you have to go on to something else. This
leaves you with two choices, each stifling enough to
promote Burn-Out: Either you go ahead and spend the
bulk of your time doing work you dislike, or you remain where you are and feel inadequately compensated
for your outstanding skills. One more "Catch-22" the
system hands out.

WHO SURVIVES THE SYSTEM?

It would be nice to think that all the things they taught us when we were young are true and that the people at the top got there because they were outstanding in some way. Unhappily, since incompetence rises, the opposite is true in more cases than not. The imaginative individual who's overflowing with original ideas and abundant energy is often considered a maverick, too difficult to handle, too difficult to pigeonhole. If he doesn't fit a particular niche on the organizational charts, no one knows where to place him, and he's passed over when promotions come due until eventually he becomes disillusioned and ceases to be effective.

Meanwhile, colorless, politically oriented hacks who make no waves and offer no criticism (no innovations, either) climb the ladder, creating a dual dilemma for their capable underlings. For one thing, there's the unanswerable question, "Why him instead of me?" For another, there's the necessity to resign oneself to working under one's inferior. Executives who rise despite a lack of intrinsic merit make unsatisfactory bosses. Because they are nervous, they are wishy-washy about making decisions, always looking to see which way the wind is blowing before they commit themselves. They are so busy preserving the status quo, they can't be relied on to back up their staff or go to bat for controversial viewpoints.

THE UNSUPPORT SYSTEM

The day Vera, the advertising copywriter, exploded, she was fed up with a boss like that. The function of a creative director in an agency is to supervise and direct a group of writers and artists, assigning the work to one team or another, discussing it with them, making suggestions, and finally, giving initial approval or disapproval to their ideas. Vera's creative director, however, was a spineless equivocator who never stuck to an opinion. Time and time again, Vera had thought they were in agreement, only to find him doing an about-face at a critical moment. She was a talented writer with her own brand of style and flair, and she had repeatedly asked to be transferred to some other group where she'd have a chance of getting her more original ideas through, but he refused to let her go because even her more conventional work was an asset to his department. She had long since given up hoping that things would change, and by the day we looked in on her, she was overflowing with frustration and tension.

That day, he let her down again. When the two of them were alone in his office and she presented the flavor script to him, explaining the reasoning behind it, he had said, "Makes good sense. Go ahead with it." Then, at the meeting, in response to the first top-of-the-head comment from a literal-minded colleague, he abandoned her completely. Vera had a right to expect him to speak up immediately, before the discussion got out of control. Either he should have said, "One minute. Before you make changes, let me explain the reasoning to you," or he should have called upon Vera to defend her position. Not that Vera was naïve enough to expect to win every time, but she was certainly entitled not to lose because of one impulsive remark. A strong supervisor would, at the very least, have conveyed a sense of being on her side. He would not have let her sit there feeling like a pariah.

What might have seemed like an unreasonable temper tantrum to a casual observer becomes understandable when you look behind the scenes and analyze the situation in Burn-Out terms. Vera was achievement-oriented. She was dedicated to being creative, not just another hack. She was willing to put forth the effort she knew was required to reach the top of her profession. Yet she was stymied at every turn by a gigantic stumbling block—namely, her creative director. Early on, in a manner typical of Burn-Outs, she had determined to lick the problem, persuading herself that eventually, as his faith in her grew, he would become more supportive and more willing to take chances now and then. It wasn't her way to go over his head and gripe about him; even when she asked for transfers, she always phrased her request to sound as if she were eager to work on other products. She never said her boss was causing her grief, even after her optimism faded.

All this inner turmoil was gradually producing Burn-Out symptoms in Vera, although she was unaware of them. She was tired much of the time, depressed and cynical; assignments were taking her longer to complete. To some degree, she was showing signs of paranoia. True, her grievances were well founded, but, in her reluctance to air them, she was managing to inflate them. Anyone who had been paying attention would have caught changes in Vera: Many days she arrived at the office looking sloppy; often she skipped lunch; she was smoking more; she didn't always hear what people were saying to her.

Vera's creative director was not the only irritant the system provided for her. There were others, any of which taken by itself wouldn't have amounted to much, but which combined, added up to a high level of stress. One of those irritants can be directly traced to the layers we talked about at the beginning of the chapter. In reality, Vera was writing her ads for the ABC Food Company, and since she had researched the product and studied its competition, she felt confident she understood what the company needed to say. The problem was, she wasn't dealing with the company. That task would fall to someone in another layer. Because of the way the system was set up, Vera had to filter her work through the hierarchy of the agency, where everyone feels compelled to make a comment to prove he's earning his pay. Many times the comment is ill founded, but if the tenor of the room is one of insecurity, it will be enough to shake everyone's faith.

This is particularly true in creative endeavors, where there are no definitive givens. A musician I know was once in a studio recording a jingle for a commercial. Six or eight people from the agency were there to supervise, and about an equal number from the client. The session had taken many hours, but finally everyone was satisfied with the finished product. Someone asked to hear it one last time, and as it was being played, a young boy delivering coffee walked into the room. He listened for a few seconds, put his package down, and said, loud and clear, "That stinks!" Suddenly there was panic in the room as a dozen professionals wondered if the boy was right and they were wrong!

If lack of support, lack of security, lack of proper channels, and lack of basic courtesy (which would have led to Vera's being consulted about her thinking) are problems in corporate life, they are probably not as debilitating as lack of time. Large organizations tend to swing back and forth between the extremes of nothing to do and no time to get things done. In Vera's incident, not nearly enough time had been allotted for the project, and she had aggravated her exhaustion by working day and night to meet the deadline. She was on edge by the time she walked into that Monday-morning review session. And she was not alone. Everyone in the room was feeling the effects of last-minute pressure. Had the meeting been held during the previous week, tempers would have been cooler, nervous systems more intact, the criticism might have been taken less seriously, and Vera might have been spared an ordeal. Certainly a few hours before the client was due was no time to be asking for revisions.

OFFICE POLITICS

Ted's Story

In general, the system is not set up for the independent spirit or the talented nonconformist. Its bias is toward the staid, compliant type who doesn't rock the boat, and the people who survive and flourish within its confines are, with few exceptions, not dedicated to high achievement. Men and women who are committed to accomplishment are usually forthright and outspoken. They don't play the political game well; in fact, they don't play it at all. When they have a gripe against a colleague, they tell him face to face. It never occurs to them that many of the people they're surrounded by are not so straightforward and might be sabotaging them behind their backs. A young patient of mine named Ted had an ugly experience in an insurance company. He had been hired straight from an M.B.A. program at one of the Ivy League schools and was oblivious to the fact that some of the older employees resented him, partly because of his gung-ho attitude, partly because they felt threatened by the firm's policy of recruiting graduate students.

At the time Ted took the job, the company was in the process of petitioning the state regulatory commission for a rate increase, and the request had to be accompanied by an in-depth report, complete with company figures proving why the increase was justified. Ted's first major assignment with the company was to assemble and analyze the figures. He got started with enthusiasm, not suspecting (as, indeed, he had no reason to) that two of the department heads had determined to make sure he didn't succeed. Ted's plan was to go to the head of each relevant department and request the pertinent information, but because he was so new to the company, he didn't in all cases know what was pertinent. He would have to depend on the department heads to alert him to any crucial areas he might be neglecting to include. When he sat down with these two men, they were ostensibly co-operative. They gave him precisely the figures he asked for, but volunteered nothing additional, thereby sending him off to work with incomplete data.

Ted wore himself into a frazzle trying to make sense out of those figures. He knew certain patterns should be emerging, but no matter how he juggled those figures, they just didn't add up. One of the other young men in his department suggested he sit down with the department heads again to check for errors in the input. He did, and when he found he had the same numbers again, he began to wonder what was the matter with him. He tried the computer, he worked by hand, and he might be working yet if a secretary he had become friends with hadn't found out what the men had done and told him. That was Ted's indoctrination to corporate life, and quite an indoctrination it was.

Everyone who has ever been part of a corporate structure has a story or two to tell about office politics: people claiming other people's work as their own; exaggerated stories of carousing being "allowed" to get to management's ears; co-workers jockeying for position at meetings and other office functions; subordinates currying favor with superiors and clients; supposed friends engaging in hypocrisy, back-stabbing, and other tactics they wouldn't think of indulging in outside of the office. To anyone who enters this world with a vision, as the individual with a Burn-Out temperament does, the actuality is shocking. He may be able to make it, may teach himself how to accommodate, but he will pay a heavy price in disillusionment, distancing, and dulling.

When a person who plays fair is responsible to, or surrounded by, people who fight foul, his Burn-Out becomes almost inevitable. So many emotions surge up inside him all at once, he has to struggle to contain them. He tries to stifle or deny his anger, he wrestles with his feelings of being taken advantage of, he even works harder at his job in an attempt to repudiate the ugliness. Should all of these fail, he may turn to a False Cure for relief, giving himself still another set of problems.

GROUP BURN-OUT

The Staff's Story

Burn-Out in work situations is not limited to individuals. Sometimes entire departments or organizations fall victim. Not too long ago, a state government, which it will be more tactful not to identify, lost seven young, socially concerned staff people in what may be termed a communal Burn-Out. It got under way when the governor personally requested the department to prepare a document for him on a highly sensitive issue that held ramifications for every state of the union. The young people were delighted. Their state was about to take a leadership position, and they had been selected to spearhead the project! They fell to it in high spirits, calling a meeting for that very evening. By midnight, when they finally adjourned, they had compiled an agenda, divided the work into spheres of responsibility, constructed a timetable, and agreed upon a list of experts to call in for consultation. The deadline for the project was a scant six months away, and since the object of it was to generate a piece of forward-looking legislation, they resolved to be ready in time, even though they realized they would have to give up their evenings and weekends. They were proud of their governor for taking a stand on what was certain to be considered a controversial issue. He would need all the help he could get, and they would see to it that he got it.

Things got under way swimmingly. For the first few months, enthusiasm remained high, and tempers cool. When there were differences of opinion, someone merely had to say, "C'mon, gang, this isn't doing much for the cause," and they'd be off and running again. At the end of three months, the halfway mark, they invited the governor to join them for a meeting to review what they had done so far and offer any suggestions and comments he might have. The governor, it seemed, was too busy. One of his aides answered for him, explaining that some other pressing matters had come up, but that the governor had complete faith in them and was positive they were doing a first-rate job. Everyone was disappointed. For the first time, there was grumbling in the meeting room: "We're working our asses off, and *he's* too busy!"

At this point, the staff members began to notice things that had escaped their attention before, like the lack of co-operation from other departments. Their fatigue was beginning to tell on them, and they were becoming downright cranky. When, a few weeks later, the governor's office refused them an allocation for a much-needed consultant, they were furious. The camaraderie, which had run so high in the beginning, disappeared as they vented their irritation on one another. There was much side-taking and bickering, with a few of the members not speaking at all. The enthusiasm that had motivated them initially was now replaced by stubbornness, as if they were saying, "Despite you, despite those other creeps around here, despite the governor himself, this project is gonna get done."

In that unhappy spirit, they finished their report. Miraculously, it reached the printer on deadline and was issued to rave reviews. Just as the governor had predicted, they turned in a first-rate job, which cast the governor into the national limelight. The issue became the cornerstone of his campaign for re-election, and for a while, the staff felt immeasurably better, even patching up the quarrels and setting aside an evening for a private celebration. The governor had still not taken the time to visit them, but he sent a personal note of thanks, and they consoled themselves with that.

When the governor won the election and settled down for his second term, the still-expectant seven waited for the legislation to be introduced, only to be disappointed month after month. Twice they wrote notes to the governor asking when action would be taken; twice they were ignored. By the summer of that year, all seven had resigned to take jobs in the private sector. The government, which can ill afford to turn away competence, had alienated seven of its brightest and best young men and women in one fell swoop. The governor was startled by the rash of resignations and never connected them with disillusionment over his failure of commitment to the issue. He chose, instead, to deliver diatribes on the undependability and ingratitude of "that generation." "To think," he would say in an aggrieved tone, "we were grooming every single one of them for an important spot within the administration!"

It is hard to know whether the governor truly didn't make the connection or whether he was trying to assuage his conscience, but whatever the truth was, it doesn't change the fact that his callousness was responsible for the Burn-Out of seven exceptional public servants. They had believed in him, and he had duped them. They had contributed their energies, talents, and personal time to a cause he had assured them was for the common good, only to find he had used their efforts to get himself re-elected. They had joined his staff, idealalists; they left it, cynics.

A FATAL COMBINATION

It is more than disheartening to think of all the ways the system conspires against the individual; it is scary. Getting from one end of a career to the other is like walking through a field dotted with hidden land mines. You never know what's going to happen next or when a perfectly innocent-seeming situation is going to explode in your face. If you overcommit yourself to such an unreliable, fickle force, you're bound to burn yourself out, just as that government department did, just as the teacher, Vincent, did. *Since Burn-Out sets in when the effort spent is in inverse proportion to the reward received, it becomes imperative to balance the equation.*

Does that mean you have to lower your standards and teach yourself to care less about your job? To some extent, yes. Howard learned to, out of his own observation and experience. Vincent learned through his therapy. The government staff, which didn't learn, abandoned their profession entirely. While it's true that reducing one's involvement may lower the quality of work, compromise is a better solution than Burn-Out. I am talking, of course, about a realistic compromise, not a giving up in disgust. Although it's not easy, it *is* possible to reach a happy medium between cynicism toward your work and thankless idealism. Detachment is not an answer; it's merely a road to numbness and inadequacy. But too much attachment breeds vulnerability.

Unless you can separate your work from your being, any criticism, any setback becomes a rejection of who you are rather than what you have done, and this is a dangerous position to allow yourself to be in. Aside from the many pitfalls we have touched on already, the work environment tends to be a replica of the family unit, and you never know when you're going to come up against an incarnation of your mean brother or jealous sister, your punitive father or seductive mother. When you are at your best, this can provoke powerful emotions. When you've diminished your sense of self by permitting your work to encroach upon your personal identity, you can be hooked into playing destructive games from which you'll emerge the loser.

Compromise isn't the only defense available to a worker who wants to ward off Burn-Out. Assertiveness is another. Vera could have taken steps to remedy her situation long before that Monday meeting. She could have leveled with the personnel director about her reason for requesting a transfer, and he might have arranged one without consulting with her boss. Unfortunately, telling the truth in that particular circumstance equated in Vera's mind with "tattling," and she was held back by a still-active childhood principle that cautioned, "In our family, we don't tell on the other guy. We solve our problems some other way." Had Vera been able to review that dictum objectively, she would have seen that it did not apply. There was no need to vilify her boss in order to make her point. She could have expressed her feelings without placing blame, saying something like, "I know I've spoken to you about a transfer before, but this time, I'd really appreciate it if you could arrange something. X and I just don't see eye to eye on creativity. He's a nice guy, but I'd like a chance to try my approach on someone else. I have a feeling I could do great things for the agency in another group."

That's not tattling; it's not accusing. Managers understand the difficulty of reconciling conflicting viewpoints, and that position would have given Vera's request a more substantive basis than the one she had been using. It is important to learn that assertiveness is not the same as attacking. We don't need to sacrifice ourselves to a bad situation for fear that if we speak up, we will be forced to injure someone else. Nor do we have to feel that expressing a grievance will get us into trouble. The government staff, had they not been inclined to nurture their righteousness, could have prevented their Burn-Outs by being more assertive.

When the governor had no time for them at the halfway mark, they would have been perfectly justified in letting him know they were putting a hold on the project until he had a spare afternoon or evening. Then, since their suspicions as to his intentions had been aroused, they could have asked him some tactfully prepared questions: "Governor, what are you planning as the final outcome for this project?" "Will we be participating in drafting the legislation?" "Are you committed to following through on this?" "Can you give us your assurance on that?" If his answers satisfied them, they could have proceeded in a positive frame of mind. If they ended up doubtful, they could have asked to be relieved of the job, which they were performing on a virtually volunteer basis, working after office hours for no extra pay. Had they been experienced enough in the ways of politics to think of following such a course, they would have created many options for themselves, including being able to confront him at a later date if he didn't keep his word. After all, seven of them would have heard him give the commitment. But because they remained silent, they never even managed to communicate to him how much the project meant to them. They learned the hard way that idealism and pragmatism are natural adversaries.

STRIKING A BALANCE

Since it is the function of the system to keep the individual subordinate and to place its own needs first in the firmament, every organization has an arsenal of weapons for keeping employees in line. The fragmentation of tasks is one way to keep people from becoming too powerful. Ratings systems and periodic reviews are another, especially since these can fall into the jurisdiction of someone who has a personal animus against the reviewee. Fringe benefits may be the most insidious tool of all. As attractive as they are in theory, in practice, profit-sharing and pension funds often tie a worker to a dreary, unfulfilling job. Once an employee has accumulated a substantial sum toward his retirement, he understandably becomes reluctant to interrupt its growth, and the organization gets to keep him for as long as it wants to.

If you understand the relationship between yourself and the company you work for, you can have a long and happy career. You won't confuse it with friendship; you will understand that much of what goes on is simply the nature of the beast and not a personal plot against you. You may have to forfeit some of your ideals, but you will gain in peace of mind. You may have to compromise your work standards to some extent, but if you develop outside interests and a well-rounded life in the manner we're going to talk about later, you can keep yourself supplied with satisfaction. What you have to watch out for is striking a comfortable balance between too much attachment and too much *de*tachment. In their own ways, one is as bad as the other, and if you're going to cut yourself a path somewhere in between, remember that it will be as narrow as a high wire and just as difficult to stay on.

This is where assertiveness can help you. Convince yourself that no matter what signals the system is sending out, *you are important*. When you truly come to believe it, you will be astonished at how much weaker those signals become. Keep the revelation to yourself. It is not necessary for anyone else to know how important you are. They are having enough troubles already. Anyway, you don't want to lord it over other people. You simply want to acquire a quiet confidence that is based on you as a human being and not on the last job you did or the one you are about to do tomorrow. If you achieve that kind of faith in yourself, you will be ready for assertiveness and able to use it in positive, nonantagonistic ways. Unless you are ready, you will misdirect it, so watch yourself. Quiet confidence doesn't crash into the next guy's ego, nor does it call forth injured responses. It does nothing more than announce, in the gentlest of tones (silent, of course), that you are a person who is entitled.

Entitled to what? Well, for one thing, not to be taken advantage of. You don't have to stay till nine or ten o'clock every time you are asked. And you don't have to feel guilty or frightened if you decide to say "no." They don't own you; they merely rent you. If you're generally co-operative—and you know if you are—an occasional "no" will keep you from being completely taken for granted.

You are also entitled to tell a co-worker you are furious when you are, and why. You are *not* entitled to keep that fury bottled up and then go home and explode at the innocent person you live with. No fair, either, bitching to a couple of office buddies for two or three weeks or abusing the object of your anger. True assertiveness means picking an appropriate time and place, then saying how you feel in a rational way.

What else are you entitled to? Acknowledgment for a job well done, even if you have to supply it yourself. Are you in the habit of going around mumbling to

yourself, "They're always taking advantage of me," or
"To hell with them. Who cares, anyway"? If you are,
that's a good habit to break. It is nonproductive and it
is not true. Who cares? You care, and well you should.
It is much more bolstering to let it be known in a light,
bright way that you did something outstanding. Your
attitude and tone of voice must be free of complaint or
resentment, and if they are, you can casually remark, as
you are gathering your things at the end of the meeting,
"Gee, it's a nice feeling to do a good job." Not only will
that plant good suggestions in other people's minds, it
will also put a good one in yours, and you won't go
around for days feeling bitter.

You will do well to make your own list of "entitle-
ments," but do it with a sense of fun. Humor will help
cut the system down to size for you and make you
vastly more popular with everyone around you. Remember, if you want to avoid a Burn-Out, heavy is out;
light is in. Any time you can laugh at something, you
reduce its importance, even if that something is yourself. Does that sound contradictory? It isn't. You *are*
important, assuredly so, but without laughter, you'll
cross over into ponderous.

You know best what to put on your list, but I would
like to suggest that you are entitled to a day off once in
a while. If you never take a sick day or a personal one,
ask yourself why. Are you too proud? Too nervous?
Don't you feel you have earned it? Are you setting
yourself up for martyrdom? Do you think someone's
going to give you an attendance medal? Or have you
turned into one of those wind-up dolls that only know
how to perform one action?

Scott's Story

Scott, a high-placed executive with a chemical company, never took a day off, either. I had asked him the
question while we were getting acquainted, and his answer had come quickly. "Take a day off? You mean,
just stay home? No. What would I do that for? I've got

a busy schedule at the office. I'd feel as if I were playing hooky." I asked Scott to tell me a little about his life, but he didn't have much to say except that everything was fine. I knew he had been referred by his medical doctor, so I suggested we talk about his physical problem. "Well, that's just it. I don't seem to have a physical problem. I mean, I've got a lot of pain in my lower back, and sometimes I get spasms that knock me for a loop. But the tests don't show a thing, and my doctor thinks it may be emotional."

Scott went on to tell me he was sure nothing emotional was bothering him, but sometimes the pain was so crippling, he was willing to try anything. I could see he was really puzzled. He honestly didn't feel disturbed on an emotional level. "I've racked my brain," he said. "My job is fine. There's a lot of pressure, but I thrive on pressure. Anyway, you've got to expect that when you get to the top." Scott had no complaints about his marriage, either. "Oh, it gets a little boring once in a while—same old routine all the time—but after fifteen years, I guess that's the way it is."

One day, when Scott came for his session, he told me he'd have to stand. His back had been terrible that week, and he couldn't sit down. "Why didn't you call me?" I asked him. "You could have canceled your appointment." "Well, I had to go to work, so I figured I might as well come here on my way to the station." I was appalled. "Scott, why didn't you stay home today and give your back a rest? You can't be doing it any good riding back and forth on a train. Besides, how did you manage to sit through a day at the office?" "I didn't sit," Scott told me, as if it were the most natural thing in the world. "I stood. They're used to it by now."

I was beginning to get the point that Scott's obsession with going to work was somehow central to his problem; perhaps not the cause, but certainly an important manifestation. After a few sessions of listening to how fine everything from Scott's children to his salary was, I decided to see if I could stir things up a bit to help Scott find the chinks in the armor. I suggested he take a day off. His response was an immediate, "Impossible! This is a bad time. I'm preparing for a big conference. Lots of things going on." But I wasn't about to let him off the hook. "Scott, your back is pretty good now. You can sit. At least take half a day. Do something offbeat. Go to a movie. Break the routine a little."

So Scott took an afternoon off and had an adventure as beset by anguish as Tom and Huck's ordeal at their funeral. First, there was the problem of his attaché case. He wrestled with that one for a full half hour. Should he leave it in the office? If he did, his secretary would expect him back. Maybe he'd better check it in a locker at the train station. But no, that would take a lot of time, and he'd miss the start of the movie. Okay, he'd take the case with him, even though he might look a little silly lugging an attaché case to a movie. He mumbled something about a client to his secretary and headed for the elevator. When he reached the lobby of the building, he remembered his morning paper. If he came home without it, his wife would be sure to ask for it, and what would he tell her? He got back into the elevator and dashed back to his office for the paper.

Notice that through all this turmoil, it never occurred to Scott to say to his secretary, "I'm taking the afternoon off. Treating myself to a movie. If anyone asks, say I've left for the day. If it's my wife, tell her I'll be home a little early."

Finally, attaché case and newspaper in hand, he bought his ticket and went in to the theater, glad to be in the darkness. He certainly hoped no one had spotted him at the ticket window, but he couldn't dwell on that because now he had a whole new problem to face: where to sit. The back was no good. They'd think (that faceless they!) he was a dirty old man. He'd better not sit next to another man. Someone might think he was gay. The picture had already started when he finally chose a seat next to a woman who immediately got up and moved. "Good lord!" he thought. "Do I look like a masher?"

All through the movie, Scott was tormented by worries. Suppose there was an emergency at the office and no one knew where to find him? Even worse, suppose there was an emergency at home? What would he do if his wife wanted to see this movie one evening? Would she guess he had seen it before? Then there was the question of what train to take. An early one would lead to questions. His regular train would mean he had to kill time some place after the movie ended, and suppose he ran into someone he knew. He cursed me at regular intervals. "What the hell kind of therapy is this, anyway?"

Fortunately, I wasn't scheduled to see him until the following week, and he had plenty of time to calm down and think things over. He was still far from realizing how hilarious the whole affair had been, but he had done quite a bit of thinking. He confessed he had acted like a young kid who had to steal something to get past an initiation. "I know I behaved like an idiot, Doc, but I was a nervous wreck. I never realized before that every minute of my life is planned. I was so tense, I don't even know what the movie was about."

Scott had had a major revelation that day. He began to see that he had lost his capacity to have fun, that he had become rigid rather than spontaneous. He had worked so hard for so long, he had snuffed out his own personal expression. He had turned into a stiff, unbending man in more areas than just his back.

How about you? Are you brave enough to go to the movies one afternoon this week? I dare you!

Burn-Out and Tradition

❧

The dissatisfactions indigenous to our career world today are particularly ironic since, in our society, people rely heavily on their work to give them a sense of identity and purpose. In the process of reducing our traditions to ashes, leaving them smoldering all around us, we also snuffed out the networks of kinship that bolstered us and reinforced our singularity. In the smaller communities of the past, which we've alluded to before, people formed their identities in many ways. They were members of a particular family who had a history in that town. Their siblings and cousins, even their parents, had attended their school, and the teachers recognized their names at once. True, that was often a pain in the neck, leading to ill-chosen comments like, "Matilda, I'm ashamed of you. Your cousin Gertrude would never have done such a thing." But it also furnished continuity and the sensation of belonging.

In towns like these, even shopping at the local stores took on social overtones, as tradesmen inquired after Aunt Bess or the new baby. Merchants put aside their customers' favorite cuts of meat or style of dress and extended them credit if they needed it. When these people walked down the street, they were greeted every few steps by someone they knew. They worked among their neighbors and friends, and everyone had an awareness of everyone else's role in life. A person's work was certainly part of the portrait, but the entire canvas was filled in, and the occupation blended.

SEPARATION OF LIFE AND WORK

Now, our lives and our work are usually distinct and separate. Either we live a distance from our jobs in sprawling suburbs where our strongest connection to our neighbor hinges on our involvement with the Little League, or we settle in a metropolis where we may never so much as have a conversation with the person who lives next door. Our sense of community involvement has diminished, and so has our sense of family, as relatives scatter to all corners of the country. Our parents may still be back home in Des Moines, while marriage has taken one sister to Dallas, another to California, a brother to New York, and us to Chicago. Postcards and telephone calls substitute for family dinners, spirited discussions, quarrels, and affection.

Even the immediate family has fewer cohesive activities. If both the husband and wife work, their schedules are often different; where only one holds down a job, the wage earner spends many hours away from home, especially when commuting is added to an already long day. A whole generation of suburban children grew up with fathers who were seldom home and who were emotionally uninvolved when they were, feeling more like visitors in their households than participants. They left early in the morning before there was any family interaction. Their activities during the day drew them into a world that bore little relationship to the one they slept in at night. They and their families literally functioned in two different worlds.

Much of this still goes on and is a great contributor to our country's staggering divorce rate. A couple who started out sharing interests and goals travel such divergent paths, they eventually have nothing to say to each other, and it's understandable. Suppose at lunch that day, the husband consummates a tremendous deal. He's exhilarated and thinks he'll take the family out to celebrate that evening. Maybe they'll all go, or maybe just

he and his wife. A quiet restaurant, a bottle of wine, a
chance for them to enjoy each other away from the TV
and the telephone. At two o'clock, he's enchanted with
that idea, but he can't reach his wife, who's either out
marketing or picking up the children. By the time he
finally clears up his desk at a quarter to six, the whole
thing seems a little less important. After his train breaks
down and he spends two hours getting home, he's not
only too tired to suggest going out, he can't even generate the energy to tell his wife about the exciting deal.

Besides, she's had her own pressures that day and is
preoccupied with those. Whether she has a career or
devotes herself to the home and children, she spends
the bulk of her time in pursuits far different from her
husband's, often with people he knows only slightly.
She senses how vague his attention becomes when she
tells him about her day, and so she compresses what
used to be lively anecdotes into a terse highlight or two.
The closeness between them begins to fade, and neither
gets the rewards they both need from each other.

If a man feels superfluous in his home, or detached
from it, and a woman feels unappreciated in the role
she's playing, neither of them will derive satisfaction
from that part of their lives. Were they still living in a
close-knit community, however, they might find compensation for that lack in the bolstering they received
from other sources. Family and friends might heap admiration on them for the part they played in the success
of a local activity. They might be esteemed for their
gardening or carpentry or charitable acts. But as the
fortification of community and extended family evapo-
rates, so does the recognition we can expect for old-
fashioned virtues. The world is too impersonal now to
give pats on the head for being a good parent or a devoted son or daughter. It isn't even set up to notice
these things.

Yet we all need acknowledgment, and since we can't
expect more than momentary congratulations for excellence in everyday affairs, that leaves work as our
most obvious outlet. Success in business or a profession
is what the world understands and gives acclaim for.

Not necessarily intrinsic success, like curing the greatest number of patients or upholding the law most scrupulously or manufacturing the most wholesome product. What the world understands is material success, the outward manifestations of achievement. The higher we rise in our careers, the more money we make, the more impressive our titles and trappings, the more deference we receive, and so our expectations from work become disproportionate to what, in most cases, it can provide.

To some extent, this has always been true for the man of the family, especially as the two facets of his life have moved farther apart. With distance, time, and the increasing competence of his wife robbing him of his authority and consequence in the household, his work became a more significant source of his gratification. It's only natural, when a person is living in several disjointed worlds, for one of those worlds to emerge as the most significant and for that one to be given the strongest commitment. When it's a world as unstable and capricious as the one we delineated in the previous chapter, Burn-Out becomes a predictable outcome. With the balancing factors of community and family position wrested from him, a man places all his eggs in a very fragile basket. Should it collapse, he's left with a terrible mess to clean up.

CHANGING ROLES

With the spreading emancipation of women from their traditional roles, this looking to work for personal aggrandizement is no longer a male phenomenon. The educated, informed woman of today who has learned to be a person in her own right is no longer content to derive her standing in the world from her husband's accomplishments. Not only has she prepared herself for a place in the working world, she has also tested her capabilities in many areas while her husband was out of town on a business trip or languishing on the commuter train. She has coped with disabled cars and pipes and children. She has played doctor, nurse, chauffeur, arbitrator, financier, teacher, buyer, football coach, hostess, and social secretary.

For all of these, she has received a casual being-taken-for-granted at home and a sheaf of articles and books berating her. She no longer wants to be an extension of her husband and children. She's ready for bigger things than being "John's wife" or "Johnnie's mommy." What's more, with the galloping inflation and erosion of the dollar, a family can scarcely get by on one salary, and so she's encouraged, on many levels, to go to work. Like her husband, she'll shortly look to her occupation for a large measure of her self-esteem, and if it lets her down the way her traditional role did, she'll be prone to Burn-Out in two areas.

Since a person's value system plays a very important role in Burn-Out, there is an inherent danger that the literature directed at women today will set up unrealistic expectations which are doomed to lead to disappointment. If a woman has glamorized work in her own mind and then had that concept reinforced, she will believe she's about to enter a world diametrically different from the one she's been occupying. Whereas her life has been composed of drudgery and routine, often with no thanks, she will conjure up excitement and variety and rewards for competence. When they fail to appear, her ideals will be shattered.

Ruth's Story

Ruth was a woman of ideals. She wanted perfection in everything around her—herself, her family and friends, the world at large. When she came to me for therapy, she was forty-three, attractive, but too gaunt and drawn. She was obviously overwrought and started talking by telling me she really didn't know where to start. "Well, what seems to be troubling you?" I asked. She blurted out, "Everything!" and exploded into tears. It took a while for her to compose herself, but once she had gotten some of the pent-up emotion out of her system, she was able to tell me about the incident which had led her to come to me. Before I relate it to you, however, I'd like to put it in context by giving you some of Ruth's background.

As I said, Ruth was a woman of ideals. In her conceptualization, the world had the capacity to be kind and giving, honorable and striving. She was fond of sentences like, "I like harmony." "I like to be proud of my work." "I like people who respond with integrity." "I like honesty." "I like to be recognized for the work I do quite apart from personal considerations."

To be fair to Ruth, we must recognize that she lived according to her precepts. She had been Phi Beta Kappa in college and had supported herself through her master's degree, even though she and Ralph had already married. She had her children while she was still in her twenties, at which time she gave up work to be a full-time mother. Since she believed that was the right thing to do, she did it without resentment, and the years she spent at home were happy ones for all of them. By the time the children were on the threshold of their teens, the women's movement had burgeoned, and Ruth was becoming eager to take a job. She talked it over with Ralph and the children and got their wholehearted support. When she landed a spot with a large, national conglomerate, she considered herself fortunate. They promised her an opportunity for growth, and she fully intended to take advantage of it.

Ruth soon found a lot of grainy spots in her glamorous career-woman picture. For one thing, she had lived in town the first time she worked; now she was commuting. For another, her perfectionist standards required that she not neglect her wife/mother role, but occasionally, she had to. A competent woman came in to tidy and cook and be there for the children after school, but still, Ruth knew they liked to tell her things and have dinner *en famille*. Ralph's career was another consideration. He was in a position where he frequently had to entertain, and he was used to having her make the arrangements and join the party. She tried to be available when he needed her, but once in a while, she'd have a meeting of her own or be out of town.

One of Ruth's major problems was the difference in mores now from what they had been when she was a newly-married working woman. In those days, married was married. Men respected that status. Now, an attractive woman, seemingly on her own, free to have dinner to talk over a project, was a fair prospect for an impulsive fling. Ruth found herself floundering in these situations, uncertain how to refuse without offending clients and superiors. She began to worry about the proper way to dress: how to look chic and smart without crossing over the line to seductiveness. She knew that a certain amount of badinage was considered *de rigueur,* but here, too, she became nervous lest some chance remark were to give the wrong impression.

She didn't discuss these problems with Ralph because she didn't want to upset him, and she treated them as lightly as she could, preferring to concentrate on all the good things that were happening to her. And good things *were* happening to her. After about four years with the company, during which she made rapid strides, the executive vice president requested her as his general assistant. It was a whopping promotion, which Ruth was assured was based on merit. She accepted at once with the proviso that she would have to check it out at home, since it would mean additional responsibility and travel.

Ralph was delighted for her, and they agreed to engage a full-time housekeeper. Ruth liked her boss, she liked her work, she felt important and successful. Imagine her chagrin when she found out on one of their trips together that her boss's intentions were strictly dishonorable, that he had wanted her more in a personal sense than a business one.

THE ABSENCE OF RESTRAINTS

Ruth had a tough problem on her hands, one that many women in business face. As far as she could see, there was no viable solution. She wasn't about to have an affair to save her job, nor did she want to work for a man who would be continually angry with her. She didn't want to be demoted for whatever reasons he might invent. And above all, she didn't want to report the unpleasantness to the proper channels. It would be too embarrassing. Finally, from this choice of negatives, she selected a firm but pleasant approach, hoping she could preserve her integrity and his dignity at the same time.

She asked to see him in his office and confronted his stony formality with a lighthearted, updated version of the old "Can't we be friends?" routine. She told him honestly that she found him attractive and exciting to work with, but that she simply couldn't jeopardize her marriage. "I know we'll make a good professional team," she added. "I'd be devastated if we couldn't work things out." That had been several weeks before Ruth came to my office, and so far, nothing had been worked out. Her boss kept her on, but he scarcely spoke to her. Often he was curt, and Ruth was withering under his iciness. "You don't know how bad it is," she told me. "Angry glances when I speak up at meetings, a brusque 'okay' when I bring reports to him for approval. I'm not functioning. I'm tired, cross at home, furious at being treated this way, and wondering why I keep on going there every day. But if I quit, I'll never find out if I was any good in the first place."

As Ruth kept struggling to make an impossible situation work, she wore herself into a genuine Burn-Out. She was having trouble eating and sleeping, she was working less efficiently, she was depressed where she had always been enthusiastic, and she was so resentful of the sexual overtones of the problem that she was allowing it to affect her relationship with Ralph. Finally, she recognized that she had no recourse but to request a transfer. This wasn't the solution she had hoped for, but it didn't work out badly, and it had the saving grace of keeping her from burning out to a level of nonfunctioning.

Ruth's story exemplifies the dilemmas that crop up when restraints are swept away. We tend to look upon freedom as the ultimate attainment, but nothing is unilaterally a blessing. The same attitudes that made it possible for Ruth to move up on the corporate ladder stripped her of her protection. As women cry out for their independence, they're learning there's a price to be paid for it and that instead of stepping into an ideal world, they are facing new sets of problems for which they've been ill prepared.

Our children find the same thing when they go off to college. They leave with exuberance, delighted to be out from under the scrutiny of their parents, only to find that many of the rules and regulations they chafed under simplified their lives immeasurably. So, too, divorce. Years ago, the world didn't give its permission for breaking up a marriage. Today, 40 per cent of marriages end in divorce; 40 per cent! Obviously, people weren't serviced by being forced to stay together in intolerable marriages. But can they really be better off in a permissiveness that leads to a 40 per cent divorce rate? Can that high a percentage of marriages be intolerable? And do people make better life adjustments after the marriage has been dissolved?

THE BURN-OUT OF RELATIONSHIPS

When young men and women started to live together freely without benefit of marriage, their parents and other members of the older generation were horrified, but eventually accepted the custom, largely because they had no choice. They even managed to find good in these arrangements: "Well, at least when they decide to marry, they'll know each other. They won't be buying a pig in a poke." So there were to be no surprises, no shocks, no fatal disappointments. Marriages would be entered into on a more realistic footing, and they would be happier. Surely, the theory made sense. If two people lived together, they were bound to get to know each other pretty thoroughly. But obviously, something went wrong. Many marriages undertaken after a considerable period of sharing living quarters have ended in divorce.

To find answers to this mystifying phenomenon, we have to look again to the underlying cause of Burn-Out: the dichotomy between the expectation and the actuality. People often pick each other for the fulfillment of certain needs. I am shy, he is bold. I'm disorganized, she'll hold me together. I am smart, she is pretty. Sometimes they're drawn to each other by a mutual interest. We both love music. We share old movies or mystery novels. While the couple is still in the heady stages of infatuation, this primary asset blinds them to whatever defects exist in the partner, but, once the bloom is off the rose, imperfections appear which seem to blot out all the good.

Since perfection was the expectation, and compromise isn't in the lexicon of a culture schooled in its right to total fulfillment, the relationship goes steadily downhill. It's not in the least strengthened by the negative support system our environment provides. With religious leaders condoning divorce, with parents tolerating it, with lawyers and courts making it relatively easy, it pops into people's minds as the primary solution to a problem. Why work on this marriage when I can start a new one? Why overlook this person's faults when I can find someone with no faults? Against this kind of thinking, no effort is made, resentment and anger grow, the positive aspect of the marriage is exhausted, and Burn-Out takes over.

MINORITIES AND BURN-OUT

I have not written about special situations faced by minorities up to this point, because I feel there is an important statement to be made about the ways minority groups in our society are affected by this phenomenon. When Burn-Out strikes middle-class blacks, it does so in much the same way and for the same underlying causes it strikes their white counterparts, except that blacks face the additional weight of prejudice. Many times, they fail to be rewarded for their achievements because of their color, or they are particularly pressured because of it, and the anger and resentment either of these situations stirs up can hasten the onset of Burn-Out and intensify its progress.

Luther's Story

Luther, an intelligent young man from the West Indies, had come to the States with his family during his adolescence. Both his mother and father worked, and although the family could hardly have been called wealthy, they lived well. A strong pride system permeated their household, and the most vivid childhood message Luther received was, "We are people of dignity—as capable as any white." This message plus a circumstance directly related to his color caused Luther to have what could have been a very costly Burn-Out.

Luther did well in high school, but decided against going on to college. For one thing, his parents would have had to struggle to send him; for another, he was more interested in earning money and going out into the world on his own. Immediately after graduation, he got a job as a data processor in a large company, where he did his work well and was generally liked. He was proud of his independence and of having a place, even though it was a small one, in such a giant corporation.

When Luther had been with the company for about four years, affirmative action programs were in full swing. His company, along with many others, was under fire from the government for not having members of minority groups in positions of responsibility—a circumstance that on the surface worked to Luther's advantage. To help get the company off the hook, he was given a speeded-up course in computer programming, a new job description, and a substantial raise. Luther was excited. Not only were his parents proud of him, but also with his new salary he could afford to marry the young woman with whom he was in love.

What Luther did not realize was that he was far from ready for the responsibilities of the new job. He had been neither adequately trained nor placed in a position where a support system was available to him. He was the one black in the department and the only person who had not had one minute of previous programming experience. Things went badly almost from the beginning. Luther was intelligent enough to know he was out of his depth, but he was too proud to be constantly asking questions. Besides, for the first time in his life, he was keenly aware of being patronized, and it troubled him deeply to have to admit that color, not ability, had been behind his promotion.

No matter how hard Luther struggled to measure up, he kept floundering. The more he floundered, the more effort he put forth, but because he was beset by inner doubts (Was he, perhaps, not as capable as whites? Was he fit only for some simple, menial task? Would he have to call off his marriage and disappoint his parents?), his efforts were not productive.

Luther's anger grew into a smoldering rage for which he had no positive outlet. He wouldn't confess his situation to his parents or fiancée, and he had no friends at work. Only one supervisor seemed at all sympathetic, but because he was so highly placed, Luther was afraid to approach him. What Luther *did* approach was the neighborhood bar. To find some relief from his loneliness and frustration, he began to drink, something he had never done before, and which he could not handle.

Alcohol stripped Luther of his restraints, imbued him with a false courage, and led him to seek revenge in indiscriminate ways.

One day, a most peculiar thing happened. One of the women in the department was working with the computer, and when she punched for an answer, out came a stream of abusive curse words. Within minutes there was an uproar on the entire floor. Who could have done such a thing? Reactions varied from amusement to outrage, and when the words reappeared every time they were canceled out, measures were put into motion to catch the offender.

As the trail began to lead to the home office where Luther worked, he panicked. If they found him out, he would be even more disgraced than if he had been dismissed for incompetence. He was afraid to tell. He was afraid to quit. He was immobilized.

One morning, the supervisor Luther thought well of came over to his desk and said, "Luther, let's have a cup of coffee, and let's go to a place where we can talk quietly." Luther's impulse was to flee, but of course he didn't. When their cups of coffee were in front of them, the supervisor spoke: "You've been looking terrible lately, Luther. Would you like to tell me what's wrong?"

Luther blurted out the whole story, which the supervisor had already guessed and was most understanding about. Not only did he assure Luther that he would never tell, he actually confessed that he thought it was all rather funny. "The important thing," he went on, "is to get you straightened out."

Within a week, he had arranged for Luther to be given additional training and to work with a "buddy" until he was more confident about what the job entailed. He also directed Luther to me, and in the course of our work together he came to see the difference between *real* pride and *false* pride. Since that time, he has had a promotion based on merit, and his career is proceeding smoothly.

When we recall that Burn-Out is largely precipitated by the pressures we put on ourselves that the world then exacerbates, we can understand how blacks in a white milieu are faced with additional stress. Similarly, women in a man's world; gays in a straight environment. Those who are in a minority often have to work harder and be better than their co-workers to gain advancement. They are also likely to be on the fringes of the various social groups that form within the organization, and if their natural tendency is toward commitment and success, they will quickly become susceptible to Burn-Out.

BURN-OUT AND THE POOR

What I particularly want to talk about here, however, is the effect slum conditions have on the poverty-stricken. In my work at drug-abuse and other clinics, I came to know scores of economically-deprived youngsters who were in advanced stages of Burn-Out before they were out of their teens. My experience has taught me that although, on the surface, the high-achievement part of our Burn-Out definition doesn't seem to pertain here, in actuality it does. When we remember the role models these youngsters have and their sense of being shut out of the mainstream of American life, we can see that often their forays into crime and drugs and numbers are desperate, albeit misguided, attempts to "make it." This is assuredly not the motivation in every case, but it is in many.

Some of the youngsters I treated had all the ingredients of our Burn-Out types. They were charismatic, with the quality of leadership characteristics that quickly placed them at the heads of gangs, but which in different circumstances could just as easily have catapulted them into the political spotlight. They were energetic; they had goals. Unfortunately, the routes available to them were one-way streets to Burn-Out, and they embarked on their journeys so early, it was generally impossible to rechannel them.

James's Story

Occasionally it was. One particularly dynamic boy, James, reached our clinic just before he turned eighteen. He was sent to us by the police after being picked up for beating up gays. His choice had been treatment or jail, so he came for treatment. James had a lot going for him. He was tough but he was bright, and he had a sense of himself as being something. At the moment, he figured that that "something" would probably be the biggest drug dealer in town, but he wasn't sure. I was amazed that James came regularly for his appointments, but he had his own code of honor, and he had made a deal.

When James was six, his father left, and his mother consoled herself with a steady stream of men. The other kids made fun of James, said he had a whore for a mother. To save face, by the time he was seven or eight, he would round up a bunch of his friends and march them down to the bar where his mother worked. Then, for the benefit of his audience, he would tell the men there to let his mother alone. "Don't you bother my mother," he would say, looking as tough as he knew how. His mother was proud of "her little man," the men would laugh, and all in all, he got a lot of approval for his tough-little-man act.

James was alone so much, he took to the streets, selling his body and pushing drugs. But he kept going to school. School interested him, and he especially loved to draw. His art teacher praised his work, telling him he had talent and could be an artist someday if he worked at it. James bought himself a sketch pad and drew constantly. When the art teacher got sick and had to leave, he was heartbroken. He waited eagerly for the new teacher to arrive, but when he showed her his pad, she accused him of lying. "You never drew these," she said to him. And that was the end of James's schooling and his drawing. His secret dream was shattered. If people believed street life was the only thing he was good for, he'd stay in the streets.

At fourteen, James was spitting blood. He had tuberculosis and was placed in a hospital. His mother never came to visit him, so when he got out, he didn't go home. He lived in a makeshift way with his gang and concentrated on being the best gang leader in the Bronx, just as he had tried to be the sickest kid on his ward. One thing about James: He was never short of intensity. He was well into a Burn-Out when he got to the clinic. His body was a wreck from his illness. He was cynical and angry. He felt that the world was against him and that people in general were creeps.

What saved James was his basic brightness, which wasn't able to deny the end he'd come to if he kept on in his current life. James didn't want to go to jail. He was positive of that. But he really didn't know what there was for him to do in the straight world. He kept saying, "I want to be good at something." One day, James confessed to me that he had accumulated a fairly large sum of money. He had it stashed in a secret place, and maybe he could use it to start a business. I never asked James where that money had come from; I thought it better not to know. Instead, I spent our time together discussing possibilities with him. Today, James owns a parking lot in Manhattan, he's clean, and he still drops by now and then to say hello.

THE PARODOXES OF SOCIETY

At the same time our society dangles the impossible dream in front of us, it sets the stage for Burn-Out by eroding tradition, banishing our support systems, barricading minority groups, and dissolving relationships. It sends out mixed messages to all our emerging groups. Women, gays, Hispanics, blacks—we tell them all they are entitled to the same rights and privileges as the rest of the population; then we take our children and move to the suburbs. We advertise ourselves as "equal-opportunity employers"; then we offer unequal pay for equal jobs. To someone buying the promise and setting up expectations based on it, the contradiction between the myth and the reality is devastating.

Not the least reason why Burn-Out is on the rise today is that our society abounds in paradoxes like these. To a generation keenly affected by the Depression, poverty became an overriding demon, and they looked to the ensuing propserity as a panacea for themselves and their children. Now that they were affluent, they could furnish their families with a quality of life far superior to what they had had. But *has* the quality of our lives improved? Has affluence given us much apart from material comforts?

In some ways, no. In fact, in some ways, it has deprived us. When a family couldn't survive unless everyone earned money and contributed to the pot, there might have been some grumbling or resentment, but there was also a feeling of being needed. The ten-year-old son who had to give up his afterschool stickball game to run errands for a few extra cents, and the teenage daughter who had to keep house so her mother could earn, knew they were essential to the well-being of the family. They didn't feel aimless the way so many of today's pampered youngsters do. Similarly, when families had to deprive themselves of most luxuries, they relished the few they managed to acquire. Now every luxury has become a right, and if we are asked to forego an indulgence or to inconvenience ourselves, say, by turning the thermostat down, we become resentful. Our capacity for appreciating the small pleasures has shrunk, and with it, our perception of reward.

This absence of small, everyday gratifications contributes to our susceptibility to Burn-Out by creating an undercurrent of dissatisfaction within us and sending us out to search for the Big Payoff. And therein lies the insidious trap: Can anything be big enough when we've been led to believe that there may be something even bigger just around the corner? It may sound Pollyannaish in a world as turbulent as ours to talk of counting one's blessings, but one of the most effective ways we can inoculate ourselves against Burn-Out is to get into the habit of noticing—and nurturing—the unspectacular good things that happen to us. This may require a conscious effort at first, since we're unaccustomed to viewing our lives from this particular vantage point, but it will prove to be a worthwhile effort, since the truth is that the Big Payoff isn't out there somewhere: It's all around us as the total of all the little payoffs.

If affluence is a mixed blessing, technology, which promised so much just a few short years ago, is certainly another. What was heralded as an era of improved living for the human race—more powerful sources of energy, new avenues to health, time- and labor-saving devices—has brought down upon us the threat of annihilation by nuclear warfare or fallout, the loss of countless jobs, and the depersonalization of many occupations. The computer has invaded our privacy and launched a thousand complications on our already complicated existence.

Anyone who has ever been billed incorrectly on a computerized form knows the frustration of trying to get matters straightened out. No human seems to be responsible for the error; no voice will soothe your feelings; no name will sign itself to a response. A friend of mine, after a harrowing mixup with the Internal Revenue Service that went on for months, finally wrote an exasperated letter addressed, "Dear Computer."

This overmechanization dehumanizes us. Man used to be the most powerful, highly-developed species. Now machines are. Not only do we, ourselves, seem to have lost control over events, we suspect that everyone else has, too. Our storehouse of stress swells to an intolerable level as we lose the sense that what we do matters, and fear that even if we live moderate, sane lives, some immoderate, insane force will manage to destroy us.

SOCIETY: BREEDER OF BURN-OUT

The striver has a hard time functioning in an environment over which he feels he has no control. As a perfectionist, he has dedicated himself to achieving a goal, and he wants to believe that whether or not he reaches it is of some consequence. If the world makes him feel too small, it will of necessity make his efforts seem insignificant, thereby adding to his vulnerability. Since Burn-Out is produced by an incompatibility in the relationship of an individual to the society of which he's a part, we had a better chance of escaping unscorched when the world gave us more agreement and support. Today, the committed human being looks around and wonders what kind of world he has committed himself to. He may be slow to recognize Burn-Out in himself, but he has no trouble recognizing it in the world around him. He can't help but be aware of the Burn-Out of the planet's energy and resources. He feels the effects of pollution and noise and the general erosion of our ecological systems. He no longer feels safe on the streets of his neighborhood or in his own home, as the growing crime rate encroaches upon his inviolability. He watches the value of the dollar dwindle and worries about the drastic reduction of his purchasing power. He has witnessed the Burn-Out of political leadership, of ethics in public life, and of morality everywhere.

In such an atmosphere, the individual has a tendency to put a shell around himself, which is unfortunate, since in so doing, he exacerbates his already growing isolation. From the beginning of time, we have had evidence that man is a gregarious creature with a need for banding together and an equal need for ritual and tradition. Even the rebels of the sixties who left home to "do their own thing" grouped together in communes and other replicas of family living. On all sides, we see people who ridicule the rituals of traditional religions following gurus or meditating or running to their astrologers.

A century ago, Emerson said, "Society everywhere is in conspiracy against the selfhood of every one of its members." What, I wonder, would he have said had he been living today? If society was in conspiracy against us in the day of the horse and carriage, how much more sinister must the plot be today? Would Emerson tell us to surrender, or would be offer weapons with which we could continue to fight back? Interestingly, he made that statement in an essay entitled "Self-Reliance." That should give us a clue as to what he might say, and I for one would be quick to second him. Every society has had its own way of being in league against its citizens, as Emerson's remark evidences. What we need to do is find appropriate ways to protect ourselves.

Combating Burn-Out

❧

Society doesn't change quickly. It lumbers along, shifting course from time to time, improving in some ways, worsening in others. Every age sees doomsday around the corner, but somehow the planet goes on spinning. As concerned citizens, we have a responsibility to see that it does, but as the world becomes more complex and the electronic media rush us barrages of dismal news, we feel less capable of making a difference. It all seems so vast and unwieldy, so incomprehensible. Our tendency is to give up trying and let *them* take care of it. Yet if we do that, we're a cinch to slip into hopelessness and Burn-Out. To maintain our sense of being more than ciphers, we must continue to do what we can, no matter how tiny it seems.

At the same time, we must guard against the other extreme of expecting overnight miracles. That, too, can lead us to disappointment, because when we expect too much, disappointment is always in the wings. So, on the one hand, we can't become ostriches. Unpleasantness and danger don't disappear just because we've buried our heads. No, that's denial taken to its ultimate level, and that kind of denial never works. On the other hand, we can't increase our frustration by looking to idealistic visions. What we must do is strike some middle ground.

If we want to secure more fulfilling lives for ourselves against the background of the world we live in, we must correct the balance between ourselves and society. We must make ourselves stronger. We must erect deterrents to Burn-Out. Only in that way can we accommodate to the realities and roll with the punches, not being so cowed by the bad that we can't appreciate the good.

One of the ways we can strengthen ourselves is by learning to acknowledge that the world *is* the way it is and accepting that fact as one of the conditions we have to live with. We can't despair over it, dwell on the pity of it, or agitate about it. None of those will do the world any good, and they will generate such pessimism inside us that we'll be stifled in our personal endeavors. As Shakespeare said in *Twelfth Night,* "That that is, is." Once we've come to terms with the nature of the world, we can make reasonable estimates about where our contributions ought to lie, and we can get on with the business of refocusing ourselves. Those, at least, are feasible tasks and ones which will produce visible results in short order.

AWARENESS

The biggest single gift we can give ourselves during our lifetime doesn't come in a pretty box or fancy wrappings. It doesn't cost a lot of money, and it may never impress the neighbors. It's a quiet, readily-available commodity known as self-awareness, and while it can't be acquired without an expenditure of time and effort, it will pay off in handsome dividends. By now, the questions and answers sprinkled throughout the book should have started you watching yourself and your behavior patterns. To succeed in averting a Burn-Out, it's imperative to continue monitoring yourself. Only *you* know when it's time for you to stop driving yourself. Only *you* can tell when your resources and abilities are depleted. You're the best judge of the gap between your wish to do and the energy you have available for the doing. You owe it to yourself to keep tabs.

Take a few minutes now to review the causes of Burn-Out and check yourself out against them. Here, too, you know best how they relate to you, so go over them carefully, reflecting on each one for a few seconds. I'm putting them in the form of questions so they can serve you better as a spur to probing, but keep in mind they are attitudes that produce Burn-Out.

1. Do you feel yourself under pressure to succeed *all* the time?

2. Do you need to generate excitement again and again to keep from feeling bored?

3. Is one area of your life disproportionately important to you?

4. Do you feel a lack of intimacy with the people around you?

5. Are you unable to relax?

6. Are you inflexible once you've taken a stand on something?

7. Do you identify so closely with your activities that if they fall apart, you do too?

8. Are you always worried about preserving your image?

9. Do you take yourself too seriously?

10. Are your goals unclear, shifting back and forth between long-range and immediate?

Once you've thought about the questions, ask yourself if this is how you want to be. Is it how you started out being? If not, when did things change? Are you in charge of your life? Or has it taken charge of you? By fostering this kind of awareness, you will eventually get in touch with that real you that you have become so estranged from, and some of your detachment will vanish. At that point, you'll be able to start rethinking your objectives and reshaping your patterns. You will begin to differentiate between your authentic goals and the ones foisted upon you by the expectations of others.

OLD PHOTOGRAPHS

In the course of the book, I hope you gave some
thought to your early experiences and to those childhood messages with which you were so firmly imbued.
Since the foundation of your value system was laid way
back then, what happened to you at that time of your
life figures strongly in your potential for Burn-Out.
You may have repressed those memories so thoroughly
over the years that they may no longer surface easily,
but there is a very graphic way to make them come
alive for you, and I suggest that you try it. Some quiet
afternoon or evening, trot out the family album. If you
don't happen to have it, borrow it from your mother or
aunt or older sister or whoever in the family is likely to
be guarding it. If you can't locate an entire album,
gather however many pictures you can. You'll be
amazed at the multiplicity of things old photographs
can reveal. Start by noticing where the pictures were
taken. Do they seem to be impromptu, snapped at the
beach, at the zoo, at picnics? Do they encompass large
groups or just your parents and siblings? Do they all
revolve around some state occasion like a birthday
party or a wedding? From observations like these, you
can reconstruct many family attitudes. You can infer
whether or not your parents were gregarious, whether
the ambience they generated was spontaneous or formal, whether they placed more emphasis on fun or ritual.

IMPORTANT: Pay attention to who is taking the
pictures. Does one person always seem to be missing? If
so, who is it, and why do you think it happened? Was
that person the self-effacing member of the unit? Perhaps your father, who spent his life doing your mother's
bidding? Next, look at the attitudes of the people who
did get into the picture. Examine the stances, posturing,
facial expressions, the positions of the hands and feet.
See who's standing next to whom, what their positions

are in regard to each other. Are they lined up like soldiers, or are they touching? If they are touching, who's touching whom? How? If someone's arm is around someone else's shoulder, does the gesture seem to be affectionate or posed?

Check the smiles or lack of them. Do you get a sense of happiness? Anger? Stiffness? Relaxation? If there *are* smiles, are they insincere or have they bubbled up from within? What can you tell about role models and relationships? Are the groupings always the same? Did certain people consistently gravitate toward each other? Is one person always in front or at the center, so that everyone else recedes? Who seems to be in? Who was obviously out? There are strong implications here of how you see yourself, whom you modeled yourself after, and whether you would make the same choice today.

Concentrate on how you look in the pictures. Were you happy or sad, self-conscious or loose? Was there a shift at some point? For example, do you seem to have been happy as a child, but not as a teen? Let those pictures conjure up images for you. Model yourself into the posture and attitude of the person you were when the picture was taken. Duplicate what you see, and attempt to get a sense of what it was like to be in that body. Encourage a memory of that occasion to come forth. Try to re-create what you might have been feeling that day. Then do the same with the other people, particularly the one who was your role model. Do the feelings you evoke jibe with the ones you're accustomed to now? Or are they totally out of sync?

In one of my therapy groups, everyone brought photographs one evening, with the agreement not to study them ahead of time, but to make their observations after we were all assembled. One of the young men, whose resistance level to admitting flaws in himself was mind-boggling, had been unable to find a really old picture, so he brought one which had been taken about two years before. Inasmuch as his marriage was on the verge of collapsing entirely and had been filled with bickering almost from the beginning, his choice turned out to be a fortuitous one. His quarrels with his wife were all based on one issue: namely, that he placed her second to his family. "You don't include me," she complained repeatedly, "and neither do they. I'm always on the outside when we get together. They don't ask me anything or really talk to me, and when we're with them, you behave as if I'm not around."

Her husband denied her allegations vigorously and refused to look at the matter objectively. But this night, as he studied his picture and described it out loud, he was flabbergasted. It confirmed everything his wife had been trying to tell him. His mother was front and center, no one actually at her side. He and his sister were together a few inches behind, he with his hand on his mother's arm. His father was a step behind the sister, and peeking out next to him was half a face—that of the young man's wife. Finally he understood. And finally he was moved to remedy matters. He declared a moratorium on visiting his family, courted his wife in flattering ways, and gave her some evidence that he cared about her. In time, his family followed his example, until gradually the breach was healed. They are still married—or perhaps *truly* married for the first time.

KINDNESS

Old photographs can teach us a lot, especially about kindness. Kindness—or the lack of it—figures prominently in Burn-Out, since Burn-Outs tend to be very hard on themselves. They're hard on other people, too, but *they* are their own primary whipping boys. By setting themselves such high standards and pursuing them so fiercely, they insure their own discontent. Nothing is ever enough; every accomplishment leaves something to be desired. They rebuke themselves constantly for not doing more, being more, achieving more. They seem to have a constitutional inability to accept themselves for what they are, and a secret belief that other people wouldn't like them if they really knew them. Hence the image, the striving, the constant driving of themselves toward some elusive something. Fritz Perls said, "Friend, don't be a perfectionist. Perfectionism is a curse and a strain." In case you've never run across those words, I commend them to you as a motto to keep in the forefront of your mind.

To return to how the photographs can help, I suggest that when you sit down with your album, you do one thing beyond what has already been mentioned: Look at that child you were from the vantage point of who you are now. Does he or she elicit compassion in you? If you see unhappiness or fright or shyness in that child's face, do you want to reach out and comfort him? Do you want to say, "There, there, you're a good kid, and everything will be okay"? *Well, say it.* And remember, that little kid hasn't vanished from the earth. He's alive and well somewhere inside of you. You can help him emerge with confidence and pride by showing him a little tenderness, by letting him see he's all right with you. ALL RIGHT JUST THE WAY HE IS.

Self-acceptance isn't self-indulgence. It's kindness, and kindness is a benign force. In the glow of its therapeutic rays, we unfold and flourish. Our strengths multiply; our weaknesses are healed. We become surer of ourselves, and so have less need to be proving something all the time. We can make mistakes with impunity, because we can forgive ourselves for our mistakes. We stop needing constant approval from others, which allows us to like them better and to be kinder to them as well as to ourselves. We regain our autonomy and we're much the better for it.

CHANGING

There are many specific steps you can take to interrupt a Burn-Out and get yourself headed toward a more rewarding life. You can reassess your goals in terms of their intrinsic worth, you can review your attitudes and update them where updating seems indicated. If you think of your mind the way you think of your clothes closet, you'll air it out every so often, brushing off accumulated dust. You'll discard outmoded notions the way you do an outmoded suit. You'll see what needs altering and cleaning and attend to it. You wouldn't wear a hat and coat just because your mother gave them to you when you were a little kid, yet you may be wearing points of view for that very reason, and they may be just as ill-fitting and ridiculous.

Scrutinize your relationships and friendships as objectively as you can, concentrating on what *you* are bringing to *them*. If things are not going too well, try to figure out in what ways *you* may be contributing. Get out of the habit of placing blame on the other. See first how much blame may be yours. Do you distance yourself from the other person? Are you stingy about sharing yourself? Are you listening when the other talks? Can you sympathize with his or her problems? Even better, can you empathize? Look for those good points that drew you to the person initially and give them fresh emphasis and importance. See if you can discover new ways of viewing the other's faults so that you minimize rather than magnify them.

Think about your work. Are you letting it devour you? Can you continue to do a good job without being so intense? Can you take a day off now and again? Can you delegate some of your responsibilities? Consider also whether you're being selfish by not turning over a share of your duties to someone else. Your overcommitment may be depriving a fellow worker of an opportunity. Be honest with yourself about your motivations for working so hard. Is there some other area of life you want to avoid? Pursuits undertaken for the wrong reasons backfire, so be firm with yourself while you probe. If it's a subject that makes you uncomfortable, you'll try to wiggle out of answering. Don't let yourself. It will save you grief in the long run.

Do a quick survey of how you spend your time. Are you doing a variety of things or the same one over and over? Have you let your social life deteriorate into nothingness? Are you cultivating new people and being

attentive to old friends? Remember, the more well
rounded your life is, the more protected you are against
Burn-Out. If you've stopped trying new activities, make
a conscious effort to start again. Dig up your old, ad-
venturous spirit and get it going. Try jogging or skating
or swimming or tennis or dancing, but try something.
You'll add fun to your routine and subtract tension. Go
on vacation to some place you've never been before.
Let your hair down. Have a good time.

Again and again, have a good time. You deserve it.
But stay away from the False Cures. They're killers.
And they're a thousand times easier to stop before they
begin. Remember, if you're burning out, you're not
having a good time. That fire, which should be burning
so bright inside of you, is consuming rather than warm-
ing you. Be dedicated; be committed—but not in a fanatical, desperate way. Here's one more motto for you,
thanks to American humorist Kin Hubbard: "Do not
take life too seriously; you will never get out of it
alive."

References

༄

Antonovsky, A. *Health, Stress and Coping*. San Francisco: Jossey-Bass, 1979.

Daley, M. R. "Burn-Out: Smoldering Problem in Protective Services," *Social Work,* Sept. 1979, pp. 375–79.

Dohrenwend, B., and Dohrenwend, B. S. *Stressful Life Events: Their Nature and Effects*. New York: John Wiley & Sons, 1974.

Freudenberger, H. J. "Burn-Out: The Organizational Menace," *Training and Development Journal,* July 1977, pp. 27–29.

———. "The Staff Burn-Out Syndrome in Alternative Institutions," *Psychotherapy: Theory, Research and Practice,* Vol. 12, No. 1, 1975, pp. 72–83.

———. "All The Lonely People, Where Do They All Come From?" in Davis, E. (ed.), *The Beatles Book*. New York: Contes, 1968.

———. "The Staff Burn-Out Syndrome." Washington, D.C.: Drug Abuse Council, 1975.

———. *Journal of Social Issues,* Vol. 30, No. 1 (whole number). Free clinic handbook.

Freudenberger, H. J., and Marrero, F. "A Therapeutic Marathon with Vietnam Veteran Addicts," *Voices,* 1973, pp. 34–42.

Freudenberger, H. J., and Overby, A. "Patients from Emotionally Deprived Environments," *Psychoanalytic Review,* Vol. 56, No. 2, 1969.

Freudenberger, H. J., and Robbins, A. "The Hazards

of Being a Psychoanalyst," *Psychoanalytic Review,* Vol. 66, No. 2, Summer 1979, pp. 224–96.

Goldberg, P. *Executive Health.* New York: McGraw-Hill, 1978.

Hall, Richard; Gardner, C. W.; Perl, M. S.; Stickney, S.; and Pfefferbaum, B. "The Professional Burn-Out Syndrome," *Psychiatric Opinion,* Apr. 1979, pp. 12–17.

Hoffer, Eric. *The True Believer.* New York: Harper & Brothers, 1951.

Mahingly, M. "Sources of Stress and Burn-Out in Professional Child Care Work," *Child Care Quarterly,* Vol. 6, No. 2, 1977, pp. 127–37.

Maslach, C. "Burned-Out," *Human Behavior,* Sept. 1976, pp. 16-18.

Maslach, C., and Pines, A. "The Burn-Out Syndrome in the Day Care Setting," *Child Care Quarterly,* Vol. 6, No. 2, 1977, pp. 100–14.

Pines, A., and Dafry, D. "Occupational Tedium in the Services," *Social Work,* Vol. 23, Nov. 1978, pp. 506–8.

Shubin, S. "Burn-Out: The Professional Hazard You Face in Nursing," *Nursing,* 1978, Vol. 8, No. 7.

Stone, G.; Cohen, F.; and Adler, N. E. *Health Psychology.* San Francisco: Jossey-Bass, 1979.

Stotland, E. *The End of Hope: A Social Clinical Study of Suicide.* New York: Free Press of Glencoe, 1964.

White, A. L. *A Systems Response to Staff Burn-Out.* Rockville, Md.: HCS, 1978.

ABOUT THE AUTHORS

HERBERT J. FREUDENBERGER, Ph.D., has practiced psychoanalysis independently for the past 25 years. He has a doctorate from New York University; he is a fellow in the American Psychological Association and twice president of the New York Society of Clinical Psychologists. He is author of over 60 magazine and journal articles and is currently serving as president of the Psychotherapy Division of the American Psychological Association.

GERALDINE RICHELSON's free-lance writing ranges from advertising copy and light verse to children's literature and serious nonfiction. She has a B.A. in English from Hunter College, has two sons, and lives in Manhattan.

MONEY TALKS!
How to get it and How to keep it!

YOU CAN TAKE ADVANTAGE OF THE FINANCIAL OPPORTUNITIES AVAILABLE TODAY USING THESE FINE BOOKS FROM BANTAM AS GUIDES

☐ 27178 **ALL YOU NEED TO KNOW ABOUT BANKS**, Wool, Cook $4.50

☐ 26977 **HOW TO BUY STOCKS**, Engel, Boyd $4.95

☐ 34613 **184 BUSINESSES ANYONE CAN START**, Revel $11.95

☐ 34475 **168 MORE BUSINESSES ANYONE CAN START**, Revel $9.95

☐ 26251 **THE ONLY INVESTMENT GUIDE YOU'LL EVER NEED**, Tobias $4.50

☐ 26068 **WILLIAM DONOGHUE'S NO-LOAD MUTUAL FUND GUIDE** $4.50

Look for them at your bookstore or use this page for ordering:

Bantam Books, Dept. MSP2, 414 East Golf Road, Des Plaines, IL 60016

Please send me the books I have checked above. I am enclosing $_____ (please add $2.00 to cover postage and handling). Send check or money order—no cash or C.O.D.s please.

Mr/Ms _____

Address _____

City/State _____ Zip _____

MSP2—1/89

Please allow four to six weeks for delivery. This offer expires 7/89. Prices and availability subject to change without notice.

Special Offer
Buy a Bantam Book
for only 50¢.

Now you can have Bantam's catalog filled with hundreds of titles plus take advantage of our unique and exciting bonus book offer. A special offer which gives you the opportunity to purchase a Bantam book for only 50¢. Here's how!

By ordering any five books at the regular price per order, you can also choose any other single book listed (up to a $5.95 value) for just 50¢. Some restrictions do apply, but for further details why not send for Bantam's catalog of titles today!

Just send us your name and address and we will send you a catalog!
